The Economist Intelligence Unit Guide to Building a Global Image

Also published by McGraw-Hill

Noël Clarke
THE ECONOMIST INTELLIGENCE UNIT GUIDE TO EUROBONDS

Shirley B. Dreifus, Editor
BUSINESS INTERNATIONAL'S GLOBAL MANAGEMENT DESK REFERENCE

Thomas J. Ehrbar, Editor
BUSINESS INTERNATIONAL'S GUIDE TO INTERNATIONAL LICENSING

Gray Newman and Anna Szterenfeld
BUSINESS INTERNATIONAL'S GUIDE TO DOING BUSINESS IN MEXICO

The Economist Intelligence Unit Guide to Building a Global Image

Andrea Mackiewicz

McGraw-Hill, Inc.

New York   San Francisco   Washington, D.C.   Auckland   Bogotá
Caracas   Lisbon   London   Madrid   Mexico City   Milan
Montreal   New Delhi   San Juan   Singapore
Sydney   Tokyo   Toronto

Library of Congress Cataloging-in-Publication Data

Mackiewicz, Andrea.
　The economist intelligence unit guide to building a global image /
Andrea Mackiewicz.
　　　p.　　cm.
　　ISBN 0-07-009350-4 :
　　1. Corporate image.　2. Strategic planning.　3. Competition,
International.　4. Corporate image—Case studies.　I. Title.
HD59.2.M33　1993
659.2—dc20　　　　　　　　　　　　　　　　　　　　　93-6485
　　　　　　　　　　　　　　　　　　　　　　　　　　　　　CIP

1 2 3 4 5 6 7 8 9 0　DOC/DOC　9 9 8 7 6 5 4 3

ISBN 0-07-009350-4

*The sponsoring editor for this book was David Conti, the editing supervisor
was Christine H. Furry, and the production supervisor was Suzanne W.
Babeuf. It was set in Baskerville by North Market Street Graphics.*

Printed and bound by R. R. Donnelley & Sons Company.

Contents

12. Protecting the Corporate Image   173

Preface

In the 1990s the quality of a company's image can be its competitive edge—the difference between success and failure in the global marketplace.

Research has found 9 out of 10 consumers reporting that when choosing between products that are similar in quality and price, the *reputation of the company* determines which product or service they buy.

While many foreign companies are beginning to wage image campaigns—in the United States they are striving to be identified as U.S. firms that boost employment, transfer technology, and are an asset to the economy—U.S. companies have been far slower to focus on the benefits of a sound global image.

In order to survive and prosper in the fiercely competitive world market, corporations are now forced to concentrate on building an enduring and positive global perception of who and what they are. In this time of falling trade barriers, *The Economist Intelligence Unit Guide to Building a Global Image* is a much-needed practical guide to positioning, protecting, and advancing a company's image *wherever* it does business.

Using examples of successful and not-so-successful strategies adopted by some of the world's best-known corporations, this book shows clearly how to develop and use a global corporate identity to further the interests of the company. Senior executives, strategic planners, marketing managers, public relations professionals, and corporate communications executives are but a few of the people who will benefit from these examples.

Chapter 1 presents an overview of the global company, highlighting the differences between multinational companies and those in the global marketplace.

The importance of the company name as part of its global image is the subject of Chapter 2. The chapter includes new-name guidelines that may help give a company a new lease on life.

It is the product's brand name, along with its "brand equity," that translates directly to business results and profit performance. Chapter 3 shows how a company might capitalize on the strength of its brands in the new global marketplace.

Using the image campaigns of Reebok and Apple Computer as examples, Chapter 4 takes the reader through the processes these two companies have used to build successful global images.

As companies evolve and adapt new strategies to meet changes in the marketplace, it may well become necessary to rework their existing images. How to make the decision to change image—even a highly effective one—is covered in Chapter 5. Guidelines for updating an old image once the decision to change is made are included.

Tinkering with the tried-and-true proved a disaster in the case of the "New Coke" campaign, but there are instances where tough financial circumstances mean that images must be changed—regardless of the consequences. Chapter 6 shows how two companies (Waterford Wedgwood and Jaguar) are handling the problem.

Worldwide concerns with the environment are challenging companies on two fronts: government regulatory policy and public activism. How to adjust to global pressures and build a friend-to-the-environment image is the important subject of Chapter 7.

Tracking developments that can negatively affect a company's image is crucial to developing an early-warning system. Chapter 8 includes an Issue Management Worksheet, developed by a global company, as a suggested framework for tracking potentially damaging issues.

Almost every company will have to deal with at least one crisis at some point in its history. (Remember Johnson & Johnson's successful handling of the Tylenol crisis.) Chapter 9 tells how management should react to best mitigate a problem and preserve its image. It stresses the need to take into account cultural differences and attitudes in handling image-damaging crises.

The concept of good corporate citizenship in both meaning (beyond philanthropy) and scope (beyond domestic markets) will expand in the 1990s. Chapter 10 explores the use of philanthropy to boost a company's global image.

The importance of corporate advertising for global companies is the subject of Chapter 11. This chapter contains samples of ads used by Asea Brown Boveri, Toyota, Honda, and Fujitsu.

Especially in the United States, boycotts have gained prominence as a means for consumer groups to express their opposition to certain corporate practices. Chapter 12 shows ways for companies to develop policies to manage their response to boycotts and thus protect the positive corporate image.

Reading the case examples in the pages that follow, a reader is sure to recognize similarities to his or her own company. Once learned, the lessons of these examples will help in establishing a company's positive global image—one that will hold the promise of success in an increasingly competitive environment.

Andrea Mackiewicz

The Research Team

The Economist Intelligence Unit's Project Team

Senior Project Advisor

Shirley B. Dreifus
Vice President & Director
Global Management Publications

Project Author

Andrea Mackiewicz
Senior Editor

Contributing Authors

Yasmin Ghahremani
Diana Sterne

Editors

Rena Grossfield
Arline Meltzer

Dunham & Marcus's Project Team

Andrea Dunham
Cofounder and Managing Director

Jill H. Kaufman
Senior Project Manager

John Kottmann
Associate Project Manager

Company Profiles

ABB (Asea Brown Boveri) Ltd.: Headquartered in Zurich, Switzerland. ABB is an electrotechnical company providing engineered systems, services, and advanced technology to the power and process industries and to the public sector worldwide. The company has 215,000 employees and operates with major group companies in 140 countries around the world. Revenues for 1991 totaled $28.6 billion.

Akzo NV: Headquartered in Arnhem, the Netherlands. Akzo is a global chemical company that manufactures and markets basic and specialty chemicals, synthetic fibers, coatings, and health-care products. The company employs 70,000 people worldwide and maintains operations in 50 countries. Akzo's sales totaled $9 billion in 1991.

Apple Computer Inc.: Headquartered in Cupertino, California. Apple is a leading global manufacturer of personal computers and related products. The company employs about 12,000 people and operates in North America, Europe, Australia, Latin America, and the Far East. Worldwide sales for 1991 totaled $6.3 billion.

BT (British Telecommunications) PLC: Headquartered in London, the United Kingdom. BT provides telecommunications and information products and services. The company operates in 20 countries worldwide and has 250,000 employees. Revenue for 1991 totaled $23.1 billion.

Burroughs Wellcome Co.: Headquartered in Research Triangle Park, North Carolina. Burroughs Wellcome, the U.S. subsidiary of the British company, The Wellcome Foundation Ltd., researches and develops health-care products. The company employs 20,000 people. Worldwide annual sales of the Wellcome Group totaled $2.8 billion for the year ending August 1991.

Dow Chemical Co.: Headquartered in Midland, Michigan. Dow manufactures and supplies more than 2000 products, including chemicals and performance products, plastics, hydrocarbons, energy and consumer specialties, agricultural products, and pharmaceuticals. With 62,000 employees, Dow operates in 32 countries. Sales for 1991 totaled $19.3 billion.

Elf Aquitaine Group: Headquartered in Paris, France. Elf Aquitaine's worldwide operations span every aspect of the petroleum industry, as well as bulk and specialty chemicals, pharmaceuticals, beauty products, and bio-industries. The company has almost 600 subsidiaries and employs 73,000. Sales for 1991 totaled $35.6 billion.

Fujitsu America Inc. (FAI): Headquartered in San Jose, California. FAI is the largest overseas subsidiary of Tokyo-based Fujitsu Ltd., a global leader in computer, telecommunications, and semiconductor technologies. FAI's divisions and six domestic subsidiaries develop, design, manufacture, market, and support a broad range of computer and telecommunications systems. The company operates over 150 facilities in 33 states and Canada, including four manufacturing plants. FAI has nearly 5000 employees. Total revenues for fiscal 1990 (ended March 31, 1991) stood at $1.5 billion.

H.B. Fuller Co.: Headquartered in St. Paul, Minnesota. H.B. Fuller produces industrial adhesives, sealants, coatings, sanitation chemicals, and specialty waxes. The company employs 5600 and has manufacturing operations in 32 countries. Revenues for 1991 totaled $8.5 billion.

Grand Metropolitan PLC: Headquartered in London, the United Kingdom. Grand Met is an international food, drink, and retailing enterprise. Operations are concentrated in Western Europe, North America, and Japan/Far East. The company employs 150,000 worldwide. Sales for 1991 totaled $15.3 billion.

Hitachi Ltd.: Headquartered in Tokyo, Japan. Hitachi is a major producer of power systems and equipment, consumer products, information and communication systems, electronic devices, machines, wire and cable, metals, chemicals, and other products. The company employs 77,981 people throughout Japan, the Americas, Europe, and Asia. Revenues for fiscal year 1991 (ended March 31, 1992) totaled $58.4 billion.

Honda Motor Co.: Headquartered in Tokyo, Japan. Honda manufactures motorcycles, cars, trucks, farm machinery, three- and four-wheel all-terrain vehicles, and lawn mowers. Honda has 46,238 employees. Revenues for fiscal year 1991 (ended March 31, 1992) totaled $33 billion.

IBM Co.: Headquartered in Armonk, New York. IBM is a major producer of information processing systems and software and communications systems for business, government, science, space exploration, defense, education, and medicine. The company employs 374,000 in 132 countries. Sales for 1991 totaled $37 billion.

Jaguar Ltd.: Headquartered in Coventry, the United Kingdom. Jaguar, a subsidiary of Ford Motor Co., manufactures luxury and sports cars. The company employs 10,500 and operates in 45 countries. Car sales for 1991 totaled 25,676.

Johnson & Johnson: Headquartered in New Brunswick, New Jersey. Johnson & Johnson is a leading producer of health-care products, pharmaceuticals, and professional and consumer products. The company employs 81,300 people and operates in 60 countries worldwide. Sales for 1991 reached $12.4 billion.

Levi Strauss & Co.: Headquartered in San Francisco, California. Levi Strauss is a major producer of apparel for men, women, and children, specializing in denim. The company employs 31,000 people in the United States, Europe, Asia/Pacific, Canada, and Latin America. Sales for 1991 totaled approximately $4.9 billion.

Matsushita Electric Industry Co. Ltd. (MEI): Headquartered in Osaka, Japan. MEI is one of the world's leading electronics manufacturers, with over 120 subsidiaries and affiliates in 38 countries. Products include video equipment, electronic components, home appliances, and communications and industrial equipment. Some brand names are National, Panasonic, Technics, and Quasar. MEI employs 67,700 worldwide. Sales for fiscal 1991 (ended March 31, 1992) totaled $46.9 billion.

McDonald's Corp.: Headquartered in Oakbrook, Illinois. McDonald's develops, operates, and franchises quick-service restaurants, specializing in hamburgers. The company has 12,000 restaurants worldwide and operates in 55 countries. Sales for 1991 totaled $6.7 billion.

Reebok International Ltd.: Headquartered in Stoughton, Massachusetts. Reebok is a major manufacturer of athletic footwear and apparel. The company employs 3900 people and operates in 118 countries. Sales for 1991 totaled $2.7 billion.

Scott Paper Co.: Headquartered in Philadelphia, Pennsylvania. Scott Paper is the largest worldwide manufacturer of sanitary tissue in the world. The company manufactures paper products, personal care and cleaning products, and coated and uncoated printing and publishing papers. Operating in 21 countries, Scott employs 30,800 people. Sales for 1991 totaled $5 billion.

Sony Corp.: Headquartered in Tokyo, Japan. Sony is a global manufacturer of audio and video equipment, computers and peripherals, electronic devices, and music and video software. The company also produces and distributes motion pictures and television productions. Sony employs 95,600 people. Sales for fiscal year 1991 (ended March 31, 1992) totaled $28.7 billion.

Toyota Motor Corp.: Headquartered in Toyota City, Japan. Toyota Motor is a major manufacturer of automobiles and trucks, with 30 plants in more than 20 countries. The company employs 97,000. Sales for fiscal year 1990 (ended June 30, 1991) totaled $71.4 billion.

Volvo AB: Headquartered in Goteborg, Sweden. Volvo's main operations encompass the development, manufacture, and marketing of transportation equipment, but also include some trading in goods and services and financing activities. The company sells its products in 130 countries and produces in 30. In 1991, worldwide sales totaled $13.9 billion.

Warner-Lambert Co.: Headquartered in Morris Plains, New Jersey. Warner-Lambert is a multinational health-care and consumer product company. With operations in 130 countries, the company employs 34,000 people. Revenues for 1991 totaled $5.2 billion.

Waterford Wedgwood PLC: Headquartered in Waterford, Ireland. Waterford is a leading manufacturer of lead crystal and fine china. The company employs 10,161 people in seven countries. Sales for 1991 totaled $5.1 billion.

Xerox Corp.: Headquartered in Stamford, Connecticut. Xerox is a manufacturer of business products and systems, including copiers, duplicators and facsimile devices, computer-related equipment and services, and information word-processing equipment. The company has 110,000 employees and operates in 130 countries. Sales for 1991 totaled $17.8 billion.

1

The Global Company

In the new global marketplace, a positive image will go far to distinguish a company. As companies reach parity with their competitors on product quality, customers will gravitate toward subjective criteria in purchasing decisions, such as, "Do I feel good about doing business with this company?" According to Opinion Research Corp., 9 out of 10 consumers report that when choosing between products that are similar in quality and price, the reputation of the company determines which product or service is bought.

Thus, a strong global image is one of a company's most valuable assets, and it should receive the same attention as that devoted to products and services. Indeed, even in their home countries, companies can no longer assume that a strong image will be enough to stave off domestic competition. Many foreign companies are beginning to wage image campaigns that identify them as U.S. companies in the United States, French companies in France, and Asian companies in Asia. Sweden's ABB (Asea Brown Boveri), the Netherlands' Philips, France's Thomson, and Japan's Toyota are all striving to be identified as U.S. firms that boost employment, transfer technology, and are an asset to the United State's economic strength.

U.S. companies, on the other hand, have been far slower to focus on global image than their overseas counterparts. A 1988 survey by Lippincott & Margulies, the image management consultants, revealed that 71 percent of Japanese executives said their companies had increased their focus on corporate identity practices abroad since 1986. This is compared with 50 percent of European and 36 percent of American companies. Nevertheless, all corporations will be forced to concentrate their attention on building global perception to survive in a fiercely competitive world market.

Although most people do not differentiate between "image" and "identity," there are differences. Images tend to be gradually perceived, whereas

1

identities are quickly observed. Moreover, images are evolutionary and are often made up as the company's business progresses. Identities, on the other hand, can be created on a drawing board, carefully pieced together, and, most important, controlled. Traditionally, corporate identity—and image as an extension of identity—focused on a company's name and graphic expression (see Chapter 2) or its brands (see Chapter 3). However, today's corporate challenge is also to build a broader worldwide image that includes these two concepts and is understood on a global basis.

Corporate image is defined as the perceived sum of the entire organization, its plans and objectives. It encompasses the company's products, services, management style, communications activities, and actions around the world. A company projects itself through the logo it chooses, its corporate name, its brand images, the messages it communicates to its customers, and corporate actions both inside and outside the establishment.

Building a positive corporate image requires skillful long-term planning. It is important to note that many of the elements that make a company global also make it harder to create and project a cohesive global image. In particular, the evolution over the last 30 years of the simple one-product company into a much more complex, diversified organization makes it much more difficult to develop a unified image.

Furthermore, as companies are expanding, they are finding it necessary to move toward more decentralized forms of management. According to the *Harvard Business Review,* 85 percent of companies are decentralized today, compared with 20 percent in 1950. While this helps a foreign company to be thought of as "local," it complicates the coordination of image-building activities. Creating a global image has been further complicated by the proliferation of strategic alliances. While many companies have merged over the past several decades, often their distinct images were either never integrated or else unsuccessfully integrated. As a result, the various parts of the company remain separate islands with different cultures and separate image-building budgets. This makes competing globally difficult at best.

The Global Company vs. the MNC

Although every company should develop a global image for marketing purposes, becoming a global entity can be impractical from a management standpoint. While seemingly similar, the multinational corporation (MNC) is not the same as the global company.

The Multinational Corporation

The traditional MNC sells to a number of countries, adjusting product offerings, manufacturing practices, and marketing strategies for each (all of which is rather cost intensive). Moreover, most MNCs treat foreign subsidiaries as distant appendages of the parent company; the subsidiaries' mission is to produce and/or sell products designed and engineered back home.

The chain of command and the nationality of the parent company are quite clear. For instance, a typical U.K.-based company operating in the United States would have an exclusively or predominantly British board of directors as well as a distinctly British outlook. The reverse would be true for most U.S.-based firms operating in the United Kingdom.

The Global Company

In reality, "many companies that think of themselves as global are really multinational," says Martyn F. Roetter, a director of Arthur D. Little's worldwide electronics, information, and telecommunications consulting practice. "Most of these firms began as local companies that became national, then expanded by selling in an overseas market or two and creating an international vice president. Some eventually moved a portion of their manufacturing overseas, attuned their products, marketing, and business practices to local conditions and hired local nationals to manage operations in key markets." Although these companies were enterprising in realizing their international potential, they are not truly global in perspective, according to Roetter, because "they are essentially a collection of national businesses."

What defines a global company, then, and why is it so important to be one? A global corporation strives to sell the same products or services everywhere and run its operations using one standard, at a relatively lower cost. It treats the entire world—or major portions of it at least—as a single market.

A global company advances on the basis of its worldwide operations. Rather than tailoring its business practices to each national market, it optimizes its strategies, operations, and financial performance for the entire world (see ABB, p. 11). National and regional differences are important—but they are not what drive the company's manufacturing or distribution systems. According to this definition, there are only a handful of truly global companies—such as Sony, IBM, and ABB. However, many other companies are close to being global.

"You could say that the global corporation knows everything about one great thing," writes Harvard Business School Prof. Theodore Levitt in the

Harvard Business Review. "It knows about the absolute need to be competitive on a worldwide basis as well as nationally, and seeks constantly to drive down prices by standardizing what it sells and how it operates. It treats the world as if it were composed of a few standardized markets rather than many customized markets. It works toward global convergence." Levitt points to the bottom-line benefits of this approach: "If a company treats the world as one or two distinctive product markets, it can serve the world more economically than if it treats it as three, four, or five product markets."

Another dimension of the truly global corporation, according to Toshio Egawa, a board member and director of corporate planning at Konica Corp. (which he acknowledges is not yet a global company), is the intangible quality known as "character." Egawa likens the successful global organization to the Jesuits of the 16th century: "The Jesuits were enormously successful at selling a religious concept around the world. This couldn't be done by strategy or by technological means. It required something of moral character, something of personality. There was no communication, yet they maintained that global organization. There's a lot to be learned from that."

In discussing Sony Corp., one of the best-known global firms, Neil Vander Dussen, vice chairman of Sony of America, details the attributes of any company seeking to become global: "We are entering an age of borderless competition. In the 1990s, we believe our company must possess four characteristics: We must be more global, more localized, more integrated, and more decentralized. These four characteristics may seem contradictory. But they are, in fact, mutually supportive." (How Sony became a global company and what it is doing to remain at the forefront of the global ranks are discussed beginning on p. 14.)

Global Board of Directors

A global company is more likely than a traditional MNC to recognize the importance of having people on the board of directors who come from countries other than the one where the company is legally domiciled. These companies have decided not only to be managed globally but also to be governed globally. They have come to realize that policies determining critical functions (e.g., research and development, capital spending, and succession planning) profoundly affect worldwide operations and require the broadest possible decision-making framework. Therefore, they have begun moving toward internationalizing their boards of directors with one or more nondomestic representatives.

Differences between Global Companies and MNCs

The Global Company

- More products sold outside the home territory than within it
- Decision making is localized, not centralized
- R&D implemented wherever necessary—often in foreign labs
- Company stock usually listed on several foreign exchanges
- Shareholders spread around the world
- Nonnational executives on the fast track to top management
- Significant number of nonnational directors on the board
- Trade barriers not a threat to business
- Multiple identities and loyalties successfully managed, in part through a fluid chain of command
- Global image bolstered, rather than confined, by strong home-country identity (if the firm has one)

The Traditional MNC

- Home territory still the major market
- Foreign subsidiaries operate as appendages of headquarters, which make the major decisions
- Research conducted and products designed at headquarters
- Company stock listed on home-country stock exchange only
- Shareholders mainly in home country
- Overseas management staffed and directed primarily from headquarters, with few nonnationals on fast track
- Few, if any, nonnationals on the board
- Decision making strongly affected by national boundaries and trade barriers
- Clear, unambiguous chain of command
- Narrow—and limiting—home-country identity

Homegrown Bias

In the United States, directors of many corporations remain largely home-grown. In 1989, of the 589 U.S. firms surveyed by the Conference Board, only 100 (or 17 percent) had one or more directors on their boards who were not U.S. citizens. "This is higher than the 12 percent figure in the 1972 survey, but the gain is not what one might expect in view of the strong trend toward internationalization of business enterprise during the interval between these two surveys," says Jeremy Bacon, the study's author.

However, as one might expect, the incidence of foreign directors was higher among multinational companies than among companies in general. The percentage of such firms with foreign directors was twice as high—33%—among the 192 companies that identified themselves as multinational.

Foreign directors were also found more often on manufacturing boards than in other industries, as the following table, based on all companies—not just MNCs—indicates. For example, of the total of 205 such directors, 133—about two-thirds—were on manufacturing boards. "This may well be because manufacturing firms account for fully 80 percent of the 192 companies with significant revenues and/or operations outside the United States," explains Bacon.

Industry	Percent of companies with at least one non-U.S. citizen director
Manufacturing	24%
Financial	14%
Nonfinancial service	9%

Respondents who have no noncitizens on their boards were asked to explain why. As indicated in the following table, the overwhelming response was, "No particular reason."

Why company has no foreign director	Number of companies
No particular reason	307
There is a legal prohibition against it (usually industry-related)	17
There is a corporate policy against it	16
No suitable candidate has been found	15

SOURCE: The Conference Board.

Bacon's research leads him to conclude, "It would not appear that adding non-U.S. citizen board members is a high priority for most U.S. companies. Just 5 percent of the manufacturing companies and 2 percent in both the financial and the nonfinancial service industry categories are considering it."

U.S. companies are not alone in their parochial outlook. With the exception of Sony and Nomura, the top Japanese firms also run their global businesses with virtually no non-Japanese directors.

Canadians and Europeans Rank High

European firms seem much more ahead on the learning curve. Nestlé, Unilever, ICI, ABB, and Fiat are among the companies that have non-nationals on their boards. According to Egon Zehnder International, of the 20 corporations in the United Kingdom with the largest capitalization, nine have foreign directors; of the 15 largest in Italy, 11 have foreign directors; and of the 20 largest in France, 14 have foreign directors.

Canadian companies were also found to have a broader outlook: Only two boards of the 20 largest capitalized corporations are comprised totally of Canadians. Although not surprisingly, most foreign directors are either American or British. Interestingly, this practice is not shared—although one might expect it—by Australian companies.

Foreign Board Membership Gaining

Overall, the emphasis on international boards is getting stronger. Even in the United States, compared with a year ago, "there is a lot more interest in having people with international backgrounds and from different countries on boards," says Jack Lohnes, chairman of board services for Spencer Stuart & Associates, a Stamford, Connecticut search firm. "This is a very topical issue. It's all part of the corporate reaction to 'How do we perform better in key international markets?' It's all part of companies forming their new global images."

Search firm executives note that foreign-born directors are able to make the proper introductions for the company in their home countries. They can also provide insight into local markets and help gauge political and economic conditions.

An example of a U.S. firm adding global input is Hercules, the Wilmington, Delaware chemical firm. (For more examples of U.S. companies with nonnational representation, see the following box.) Hercules recently announced that Manfred Caspari, an economist retired from the German government and European Community (EC) posts, is now a board member. "We wanted someone with a different outlook," says Robert Hessler, director of financial relations for Hercules, which looks to Europe for nearly one-quarter of its sales.

Not as Easy as It Sounds.   Despite the positive effects of having foreign nationals on your board, it is not quite that simple. Time, distance, and scheduling conflicts all pose problems for companies that pursue foreign board members.

In the United States especially, cross-border differences in corporate governance and a lack of familiarity with laws governing U.S. business make recruitment of foreign directors difficult. This is complicated by the current controversy in the United States over board of directors' liability. Abraham Nad, publisher of the newsletter *Directorship,* notes that foreigners are not always enthusiastic about joining a U.S. board. "As the liability issue grows, I'm afraid their enthusiasm may only lessen," he says.

Ted Jadeick, a partner in the executive recruiting firm Heidrick & Struggles, agrees. "It's hard work to get good U.S. directors—and nonnational directors are twice as difficult." Be that as it may, Jadeick is still optimistic about his clients' commitment to finding directors who can add international expertise. He cites a Chicago firm that entered into an intense search for a foreign director. What was sought was a president of a U.K. company with $4–5 billion in revenues who would be willing to fly to Chicago the requisite 10 times a year for board meetings. Jadeick envisions more of these requests as the 1990s progress.

One way to get around the logistical problem of traveling time is to look for retired government officials or executives. "It's very tiring to fly around the world 10 times a year for board meetings. In addition, the executive loses three workdays for one three-hour meeting," says Jack Lohnes. His firm finds that many good candidates for the nonnational board position decline because of the time constraints.

With advances in travel and telecommunications, however, the logistics problem may work itself out over the next decade. Electronics may provide a solution, bringing foreign directors to a company's boardroom without having to be there physically. Some companies already have ways of lightening the travel load. The Barnes Group, for example, a metals-part manufacturing company based in Bristol, Connecticut, has one board member from Mexico and another from the United Kingdom. Because of the travel difficulties, the two foreign directors usually attend only four out of the customary 10 board meetings a year.

What are the best ways for a company to go about searching for a nonnational for its board? Basically, it should

Foreign Nationals on U.S. Company Boards

Abbott Laboratories
Sir Bernard Hayhoe
Member of Parliament
United Kingdom

Aluminum Co. of America
Sir Arvi Parbo
Chairman
Western Mining Corp. Ltd.
Australia

Campbell Soup Co.
Richard E. Harrison
Retired Chairman
Canadian Imperial Bank
 of Commerce
Canada

Citicorp
Dr. Mario H. Simonsen
Vice Chairman
Brazilian Institute of
 Economics
Brazil

Digital Equipment Corp.
Arnaud de Vitry
Chairman and CEO
Eureka SICAV
France

Du Pont Co.
Charles R. Bronfman
Cochairman
Seagram Co. Ltd.
Canada

Edgar M. Bronfman
Chairman and CEO
Seagram Co. Ltd.
Canada

The Hon. E. Leo Kolber
Chairman
Claridge Inc.
Canada

Emerson Electric Co.
Robert B. Horton
Chairman and CEO
British Petroleum Co. PLC
United Kingdom

Exxon Corp.
Sir Hector Laing
Chairman
United Biscuits
 (Holdings) PLC
United Kingdom

IBM Corp.
Fritz Gerber
Chairman
F. Hoffman-La Roche &
 Co. Ltd. and Zurich
 Insurance Co.
Switzerland

Helmut Sihler
Chairman and CEO
Henkel KgaA
Germany

ITT Corp.
Michel David-Weill
Senior Partner
Lazard Freres & Co.
France

McDonald's Corp.
Gordon C. Gray
Chairman
Royal Le Page Ltd.
Canada

Merck & Co. Inc.
Dr. Jacques Genest
Consultant
Clinical Research Institute
 of Montreal
Canada

Philip Morris Cos. Inc.
Dr. Jose A. Cordido-
 Freytes
Betancourt, Cordido and
 Assoc.
Venezuela

Procter & Gamble Co.
Walter F. Light
Retired Chairman
Northern Telecom Ltd.
Canada

Sara Lee Corp.
Baron Gualtherus
 Kraijenhoff
Chairman, Supervisory
 Council
Akzo NV
Netherlands

J. Dean Muncaster
Retired President and
 CEO
Canadian Tire Corp. Ltd.
Canada

Schering-Plough Corp.
Heine J. Kruisinga
Former Member of Board
 of Managing Directors
Akzo NV
Netherlands

Tenneco Inc.
Sir David Plastow
Managing Director and
 CEO
Vickers PLC
United Kingdom

**United Technologies
 Corp.**
Pehr G. Gyllenhammar
Chairman and CEO
AB Volvo
Sweden

Upjohn Co.
William D. Mulholland
Chairman and CEO
Bank of Montreal
Canada

SOURCE: Egon Zehnder International Inc., 1990.

- Look to members of its own advisory boards.

- Use the same networking system that it employs for finding national members—only expanded to international contacts.

- Establish a set of requirements (does the company need a person with governmental influence or one with particular technological expertise?).

- Determine which nationality may be preferable (for instance, if the company is listed on the exchange of another country, it may want an individual who can represent the views of those shareholders).

Staffing

Retaining a staff that is both dedicated to the concept of the global company and able to operate in a global environment is crucial. As the company reshapes itself into an organization without geographic boundaries, management will have to be open to identifying, understanding and adapting the business world's best ideas and management practices. Managers will be required whose combined skills and experience enable them to oversee international flows of goods, people, technology, information, and financial resources, and who understand the institutions that affect these areas. Such managers are rare.

"I think there are very few people around who feel absolutely comfortable operating in different cultures," says Arthur D. Little's Roetter. "For example, in the United States, if you don't respond to a question immediately, the silence would be interpreted as not knowing the answer. In Japan, it's perfectly acceptable to respond slowly to a question or a comment. In fact, performing quickly is not necessarily seen as a positive thing."

Although expatriate executives (including third-country nationals) are not a new concept, as companies compete globally, even more executives will be crossing borders. Such assignments will not be just brief detours, as was often the case in the past, but substantial phases of executives' careers. The trend is particularly pronounced in Europe, where plans for a unified market after 1992 are spurring companies to reorganize and shift management responsibilities from the national to the pan-European level. But even as companies are seeking a broader, Europe-wide perspective, they also want to stay in touch with local tastes. Managers are needed who can see the big picture while taking into account local nuances.

"You need as much cultural mix, diversity, and experience as possible if you are running a global company," says Bob Poots, personnel director for the European division of London-based Imperial Chemical Industries

(ICI). ICI's executive ranks were predominantly British 20 years ago; today only 74 of the company's top 150 executives worldwide are British.

Many management experts believe the Japanese will find it particularly challenging to create this sort of multicultural global corporation. Although Japanese firms are unquestionably skilled at discovering the needs and wants of market segments, the high value the Japanese place on a homogeneous work force often gets in the way of true globalization. It does not yet appear that most Japanese companies are ready to allow foreigners substantial responsibility and authority within their corporate hierarchies.

"Intellectually, they recognize the problems and challenges of being global, but today most of the development decisions are made in Tokyo, not in local markets," says Roetter. He points out that most Japanese overseas investment has been in assembly plants, with the more sophisticated design and manufacturing work kept close to Tokyo.

Even some Japanese managers are inclined to agree with Roetter's view. Konica's Egawa says, "Our society is very homogeneous, and there are established procedures, traditions, and criteria that everyone accepts. When it comes to coexisting with different value structures, the Japanese have problems. To be an exporter is relatively simple, but to manage overseas manufacturing or R&D operations is much more difficult."

Case Example

ABB (Asea Brown Boveri): "One Plus One Equals More than Two"

ABB is a sprawling international conglomerate with a truly global vision. Formed in 1988 by merging the Swedish Asea AB and the Swiss BBC Brown Boveri Ltd., in the three years since the merger, ABB has become a leading electrotechnical company, with international sales of power plants, railroad equipment, and industrial equipment of $25 billion.

Indeed, the main reason behind the merger was the recognition by both Asea and Brown Boveri that they needed a larger global presence to survive. ABB's Deputy CEO Thomas Gasser believes that "without the merger, which has given us our global power, under no circumstances would we be as successful as we are today. I think that in our case, one plus one equaled far more than two. The fact that we had the profit improvement we showed in the past three years is certainly due in part to the fact that we had a favorable market. But even more, it's the result of the actions we were able to take as a single, global company. We have been far more competitive together than we were individually."

The two companies combined are as large as their biggest competitors. They have acquired market coverage in areas of the world they did not have as individual companies, and the pooling of financial

and R&D resources has allowed them to gain a solid presence in the
United States (one of the main reasons behind the merger).
Furthermore, ABB is now an industry giant within the all-important EC.

The Global/Local Tradeoff.   Gasser explains what "global" means to
ABB: "It is wrong to say that because we're global, we're uniform. The
world is too different and human beings are too diverse. You need to
adapt to their individual needs. ABB is global because it is worldwide in
terms of presence. The world is our market, this is where we have our
people, where we produce, where our resources are."

But in terms of detailed strategies for products, markets, people, and
resources, the company adapts as much as possible to local needs. It
considers itself "multidomestic." As Gasser comments, "It's important in
many of our markets to project a distinctive national profile. We have to
be a Finnish company in Finland, a German company in Germany, a
Swiss company in Switzerland and a U.S. company in the United States.
It's how well you bridge the differences that makes you successful."
Nevertheless, Gasser recognizes that staying local and thinking global at
the same time "is difficult because there are built-in contradictions."

For instance, in one segment of the company's business, power
generation, there was duplication of effort by two large factories in
Germany and Switzerland. However, ABB decided against closing either
one because that would have meant—in addition to many other
negative factors—losing its status as a local producer in one of the
countries, and thus might have cost it local market share. Instead, the
two factories now specialize, with each one making half of the final
product. The result is higher overall productivity and elimination of the
rivalry that used to exist between the two plants.

Gasser explains: "It used to be that whenever Brown Boveri got an
order, the first question asked internally was, 'Is this an order for
Switzerland, or is this an order for Germany?' Today it's an order for
both. There were many similar situations in other business areas."

However, Gasser cautions that this type of integration takes time and
is not without its difficulties. A case in point: In the preceding example,
while the company as a whole benefited from cooperation between the
plants in Switzerland and Germany, both plants "felt that they were now
dependent on someone else, in a negative sense. They also felt they
were no longer 'complete producers.'" The pride associated with a
finished turbine leaving a factory was suddenly gone. Instead of focusing
on the positive aspects of global cooperation, people were talking too
much about what they had lost. Furthermore, in some other instances,
the merged ABB was asking people to work together who had been
longtime competitors.

The company, therefore, had to work very hard to bridge the
psychological hurdles associated with regional or nationalistic attitudes.
Gasser believes it was well worth it and that ABB so far has been
successful in implementing the change. He notes that the success in the

market shows that instilling "global pride" was the right course and deserving of the time and effort.

Managing the Global Company.   ABB's management takes a proactive approach to cementing a global corporation. "The management of a business area [there are 65 such areas at ABB] should be multinational," explains Gasser. "There should be individuals of several nationalities on a management team. In addition, when a project team or a task force is set up to deal with a problem that is international in scope, we try to have people from various countries represented, not just the ones who speak the same language as the team leader."

ABB's board of directors contributes to its global image. The board is made up of two Swedes, two Swiss, two Germans, one Luxembourger, and one American. "The board certainly reflects our own business makeup," says Gasser.

At lower levels, too, the company values international interchange. It encourages midlevel managers to gain experience abroad during the early or middle stages of their careers. "We feel that the more experience people have in working together with others of different nationalities—getting to know other markets and surroundings—the better the company's global philosophy, strategy, and actions will be integrated locally," Gasser notes.

To further facilitate the company's global cohesiveness, English is the firm's official language. Gasser explains: "Obviously if you go to a factory in France, people speak French, but if you move up in the hierarchy, there's a certain point where everyone speaks English. And when you look at any dealings across borders in a business area, people will automatically speak and write English. It has since become a part of the educational process in our company. If someone wants to get ahead, regardless of his specialty, he knows he must be able to speak English." The practice dates back to when Asea and Brown Boveri first began merger talks. The companies found that English was the common second language spoken throughout the two Groups.

Boosting Global Performance.   Although the company does strive to minimize national rivalries and promote cooperation, it also compares similar operations across borders and encourages healthy competition for greater efficiency. "You can measure and compare the productivity and efficiency of two factories and learn from each other," says Gasser. "You can go to your neighbor and find out why he's so much more efficient than you are. Why is his output per manufacturing hour 40 percent higher than yours? Why are his quality assurance costs half your own? How can he produce using only half the space that you have? Inasmuch as everyone can help the other and exchange useful ideas, each contributes to the benefit of the group. It creates an interchange of ideas to solve common problems. This creates more coherence and fraternity among people."

Difficulty arises, though, when higher efficiency leads to fewer jobs. "For example, a factory in Germany exports certain products to the Far East. Now the German costs are rising, the Deutschemark is becoming stronger and competitiveness drops. Finally, the group decides it can't supply that product from Europe anymore and will make it locally.

"As a result, the Europeans have to transfer know-how to the Far East. They obviously have the impression they are putting themselves out of a job. It then falls to management to make the employees understand that their jobs were threatened by economic forces, that unless the company took this action, there would be no sales at all in the Far East. This is the difficult side of globalization. It allows you to adapt to a worldwide shift in competitiveness, but it does not make you immune from dislocation of jobs. Communicating these messages is very important, but also very difficult."

Case Example

Sony: Global Management Drives a Global Image

Beginning in the late 1950s, Sony's drive for world market share escalated. Initially, it focused on the United States, in line with its philosophy of "Succeed first in the United States, bring back the reputation to Japan, then spread out to Europe and other countries." This strategy worked well during the 1960s and the 1970s as Sony established sales subsidiaries in the United States and Europe.

In the early stages of worldwide expansion, control mechanisms were virtually nonexistent and consisted primarily of a unified accounting policy. Everyone was so busy keeping up with a rapidly expanding business that no time was spent establishing rules or procedures. Each sales subsidiary reported directly to headquarters, with little communication between subsidiaries. Gradually, Japanese expatriates who established the sales offices were replaced by local managers who were more familiar with selling in the domestic market.

Although by the end of the 1970s half of Sony's sales were international, most manufacturing was still done in Japan. However, in a defensive move against trade protectionism, the company did build a color TV plant in the United States in 1971 and in the United Kingdom in 1973. (In hindsight, these were bold decisions, since the exchange rate was ¥360:$1 at that time, and most MNCs were relocating production bases to Asian countries in pursuit of lower cost.)

Readjusting the Organization.   At the start of the 1980s, business conditions deteriorated and revealed various weaknesses in Sony's strategy. Price competition in the consumer electronics market was becoming severe as competitors caught up in technology and companies from newly industrialized economies (NIEs) joined in the race as low-cost suppliers. Furthermore, the world economy was moving toward recession. Sony's earnings plunged steeply in the early 1980s, leading to a total review of the company's operations in 1983.

The analysis disclosed several problems. First, over 80 percent of Sony's business was in the maturing consumer electronics market, so the company lacked alternate sources of revenues to offset market fluctuations. Second, production was still concentrated in Japan even though more than three-quarters of sales were overseas. This had the double impact of making the company vulnerable to worldwide recession while putting it into a weak cost position because of the appreciating yen. Third, Sony's decentralized management approach lacked an effective control mechanism for times of crisis. Among other things, this resulted in excess inventory at some subsidiaries and insufficient inventory at others.

To rectify the situation, Sony totally revised its business strategy. The first order of business was to diversify the business portfolio to deal better with market fluctuations. In the audiovisual field, more emphasis was placed on industrial and professional markets, reducing dependence on consumer products. Numerous projects were also initiated to build the component, computer, and communications segments into future pillars of the company. As a result of this diversification, product divisions increased from 6 in 1983 to 20 in 1990.

Globalizing Management.   Changes were also undertaken on the management side, the most significant being in the accountability given to the product divisions. Previously, a product division's responsibility ended with shipment from the plant. Product divisions were primarily evaluated on the basis of sales to subsidiaries and not on a consolidated basis (i.e., sales from subsidiaries to local dealers or customers). Sales subsidiaries, in turn, were responsible for external sales. This meant that the product divisions pushed hard for favorable transfer prices without sufficient concern for redesigning products to meet market demands or developing a manufacturing and inventory system that kept stock in the sales offices to a minimum.

Under the new system, product sales were measured on a global basis. Reporting responsibilities were streamlined and centralized control mechanisms and evaluation criteria were implemented. A matrix structure was developed whereby worldwide business was the responsibility of product divisions and geographical territory responsibility devolved to country sales organizations. Although management became much more systematized, local managers still retained a fair amount of autonomy. The overall system was designed so that the different parts of the company could communicate concerns and work together to improve profit margins.

Sony of America's Vander Dussen believes that the company's form of decentralization is essential if it is to fully realize the benefits of globalization, localization, and integration. "Decision making must devolve to the company's local operations and even within those operations, as far down the organization as possible," he says. "Our local operations must also continue to develop their vendors and their employees with equal energy. As their capabilities mature, they contribute not only to local profitability—but to our operations in other markets as well."

Benefits of Reorganizing.   Indeed, the benefits of this philosophy were borne out almost immediately by the reorganization. Dialogue began between product divisions and sales companies over product innovation instead of transfer pricing. Market needs were reflected in better product design. Channel strategy, promotion and advertising, marketing investment and expense control, and inventory levels at the sales subsidiaries all became matters of direct interest to the product divisions at headquarters. Information flow among units increased dramatically, opening up both formal and informal communication lines. The process of solving conflicts served as a valuable vehicle for improving understanding among units.

The reorganization also played a critical role in shaping Sony's manufacturing operations. In the late 1980s, trade friction and competition pushed Sony into further foreign sourcing and production. Since product managers were held accountable for global manufacturing operations, the transfer of manufacturing to plants in other countries could be accomplished relatively smoothly.

The Global Mind-Set.   Nevertheless, it is clear that the reason Sony's organization works so well is not only because of the control mechanisms or the reporting systems that were put in place. Rather, it is the mind-set of cooperative global effort that has become instilled in the product managers. This has made the company immensely successful and is leading the way for it to develop new products and distribution methods and to strengthen its market share further. As Vander Dussen notes, "Technology and customer needs will change so rapidly in the coming decade that companies must have highly integrated functions to keep pace. On both a global and a local basis—but particularly in the different local operations—the engineering, manufacturing, marketing, and customer service functions must work closely together."

According to Vander Dussen, the company believes "it must continually expand its technological horizons and diversify its pool of expertise worldwide" to stay competitive. Furthermore, he notes that Sony can "improve its responsiveness in the 1990s by encouraging local talent, while promoting global interchange and cross-fertilization of these capabilities."

2
What's in a Name?

As multinational corporations (MNCs) analyze their global image, they should keep in mind a deceptively simple but important marketing tool: their corporate name. "Naming issues are rapidly becoming strategic issues," says Naseem Javed, president of ABC Namebank International, a New York–Toronto-based image firm that for over 12 years has been providing naming solutions worldwide to such corporate clients as IBM, Bell-South, Honeywell, Texaco, and Tandy/Radio Shack. He adds, "Names are created to sell—otherwise you'd simply give a company a number instead of a name. Without an effective means to brand products, services, and new or merged entities, a corporate organization could quickly find itself in a costly and dangerous stall."

Revamping an Image

When the name is well chosen, says Javed, it can give a firm a new lease on life. International Harvester, for example, adopted the abstract and future-oriented moniker "Navistar Corp."—and lost the connotation of being a debt-ridden farm-equipment manufacturer. US Steel became USX Corp. to deflect its image as a beleaguered steel manufacturer. Not all name changes are so successful, however. Korea-based Daewoo Motors provides the classic example of a campaign that backfired while promoting an unusual name in the U.S. market. "It cost them millions of dollars for an advertising blitz that relied on the tag line 'You know who, Daewoo,' " says Javed. "The result is that they are known, if at all, as the 'you know who' company."

Conveying the Global Image

One of the main reasons behind the new look at names is the emergence of the global economy. In 1955, only 34 of the *Fortune* 500 companies used coined names (e.g., Xerox or Kodak). Today that number has reached 110 and continues to increase, according to a recent study by ABC Namebank. The study predicts that by 2000, half of the *Fortune* 500 will have coined, or manufactured, names.

Such names often make it easier for a subsidiary's products and services to be identified with the parent organization. "The biggest advantage with coined names is that they don't have to be translated, a big plus in today's global market," says Javed. Moreover, companies with such names usually don't have to worry about their names carrying negative connotations in other cultures. Irish Mist, for example, stopped marketing its liquors in West Germany when it realized that "mist" means "manure" in German.

Ideally, a coined name should contain no more than four or five letters— "Exxon," for instance. However, the popularity of names of this length is making it tougher to come up with five-letter names that are easily pronounced, not already registered, or mistaken for others already in use. "This has forced many companies to manufacture names with six or seven letters," says Javed, "and many are sacrificing pronunciation."

Some 20 years ago, most products exported to the U.S. market by Japanese and Far Eastern manufacturers had distinct, English-sounding names, such as Sony, Sharp, and Panasonic. As innovations in product development and manufacturing made these brand names synonymous with quality in most international markets, management began to seek Japanese or Far Eastern-sounding names for electronic consumer products. For example, Atari, a U.S. company, was creatively named to suggest Japanese advanced technology quality to video-game customers. Korean and Taiwanese manufacturers such as C. Itoh, Samsung, Hyundai, and Fujitsu are all comfortable promoting foreign-sounding non-English names in the United States and Europe. As the year 2000 approaches, the number of Far Eastern-sounding names on the global scene will grow.

Difficult Names to Globalize. Some corporate names are less successful than others in conveying a global image. Care should be taken when considering the use of the following:

- *Geographic names.* Names reflective of their geographic roots are difficult to move transglobally. Geographic limitations are implied, a potential liability for a globalizing concern. In addition, names that are relevant only to certain regions of the world are difficult to transfer across borders. In the United States, "Federal Express" conveys a fast, nationwide courier service, but when the company began to expand internationally the name was not effective, since "Federal" is a distinctly U.S. coinage. "As a result, Federal Express acquired Flying Tigers to create a global image," says Javed. "Federal Express itself is positioned as a local U.S. service."

Of course, there are exceptions to this rule. American Express, for example, became concerned a few years ago that its corporate name was too parochial and reflective of a single-nation corporation. It did not think the name supported the worldwide financial image it wished to reflect. However, research at image consultant Lippincott & Margulies revealed that the name "American Express" was one of the company's most valuable assets. It had come to symbolize membership in an international elite and moved well beyond the literal dictionary definition of the words themselves. In fact, what was found wanting was a strong visual identity. The solution Lippincott & Margulies devised was the now famous "blue-chip" logo and a formal design and nomenclature system. Fully implemented on a global basis, this system enables American Express to leverage its powerful name while differentiating its many divisions, activities, products, and services. At the same time, the blue-chip logo is a reassuring and familiar symbol with immediate recognition in any language, in any country.

- *Family names.* The family name as corporate identifier is also on the decline. Originally, many businesses—especially in the United States— were named after the founder (e.g., Heinz, Gillette, Singer, Ford, and Firestone). Today, major corporations are more likely to be managed by a team of professionals than dominated by a visionary founder.

  There are potential liabilities when a family surname is used: The death of the founder can cause confidence in the company to drop (as happened with Ford Motor when Henry Ford died). Even an orderly succession of management power from father to son (as in Wang computer) can unsettle both investors and customers. Canadian Robert Campeau's personal and corporate financial problems resulting from his takeover of the Federal and Allied retail empires dramatically illustrate the difficulties associated with using a surname for corporate identity.

- *Descriptive names.* Descriptive and dictionary names are also decreasing in popularity because they may become unrelated to a firm's evolution. Today's Union Carbide has little to do with carbides. At present, descriptive names most often appear in emerging industries, such as robotics (e.g., US Robotics) and biotechnology (e.g., Biogenics).

The New-Name Guideline

Alan Siegel, chairman and CEO of Siegel & Gale, the New York-based corporate-identity arm of Saatchi & Saatchi Advertising, suggests the following rules of thumb for MNCs considering a name change or modification:

- Don't throw away established names unless absolutely necessary. It is frequently easier to build new identities around well-known names than around new ones. "I'm not sure, for instance, that replacing Burroughs and Sperry with Unisys was such a good idea," says Siegel, "especially as the combined company will continue in information and defense systems—two businesses where they were both well known and in which they excelled."

- Avoid using a fabrication when choosing a new name. Don't overlook names the company already owns or uses for subsidiaries or brands. But be aware that there are traps in substituting a well-known company or brand name that is associated with a specific product or weak name. "When Consolidated Foods adopted Sara Lee, it brought instant recognition," says Siegel. "But now the company has to overcome the strong association with cakes and pastries. It also makes Hanes hosiery and Electrolux vacuum cleaners. Consolidated Foods merely traded one identity problem for a bigger one."

- Don't get overly caught up in the logic, potential appeal, and uniqueness of a fabricated name. Take the time and money to evaluate it and the alternatives through meaningful research, particularly with employees, who are the most discriminating audience. "I can't believe that names like Allegis [the renamed but not long-lived holding company of United Air Lines], UNUM [a contraction of Union Mutual], and Trinova [formerly Libby-Ownes-Ford] were properly tested," says Siegel. "If they had been, they wouldn't have seen the light of day."

- Don't fall into the multiple-name trap. It is frequently advantageous to combine two or more well-known names to secure instant recognition, maintain continuity, and gain employee acceptance. "Companies such as Morton Thiokol and SmithKline Beckman have done it successfully," says Siegel. "But there are many instances when it pays to bite the bullet and adopt the strongest name. The merger of Baxter Travenol Laboratories and American Hospital Supply in 1985 could have resulted in BaxAm or BaxSup. Instead, management chose Baxter for the new name."

- Don't write off initials for a corporate name. While they are not the preferred solution, companies often find that initials work better than anything else. "Many people overlook the fact that some of the best-known companies in the world are GM, IBM, and GE," says Siegel. "I wouldn't, however, recommend initials unless a corporation has large resources to promote the name."

- Don't hold naming contests. Competitions for employees or the general public may generate publicity, but they will also end up creating problems. "You get mountains of names, most of which are useless," says Siegel. "If you end up not using a name developed by employees, you create a lot of bad feelings. This just isn't the way to handle a complex corporate problem."

What's in a Name?

What, then, constitutes a good global name? According to ABC Namebank, several elements ensure the effectiveness of a name. A name must

- Be distinct, powerful, memorable and unique.
- Communicate at least one corporate image goal.
- Be linguistically sound and transcultural.
- Be futuristic in style and international in scope.
- Appeal to the customer.
- Reflect creativity and arouse curiosity.
- Be proprietary, so that it can be used internationally.
- Be free and clear of legal threat.
- Be free of negative connotations or potential "new meanings."

Developing a Name

To come up with a new corporate image, an infrastructure should be put in place to facilitate the process. A "naming" policy and a committee with specific responsibilities made up of key people from the organization are often important prerequisites. In addition, a data base can be used to come up with new, appropriate names.

Javed believes that a four-stage process—generate, analyze, investigate, and register—is crucial in generating a new corporate identity:

- *Generate.* This is the creative stage. But in order to generate names successfully, input must include linguistic knowledge, historic name references, and an update on current naming trends.

- *Analyze.* The suitability of the name must be judged relative to desired market positioning. Consider appropriateness to company goals, competitive strengths, potential graphic applications, and modulation capability.

- *Investigate.* It is crucial to ensure that the proposed name is not in use or planned for use by any competitor. A strict checklist must be developed to make sure jurisdictions are not overlooked, conflicts and similarities are noted, and resultant search reports are prepared for the legal department.

  It is difficult to find a name that is not at least partially in use. The following are names currently being used by corporations:

Systems	173,000
Info	26,000
Tech	17,000
Micro	11,000
Royal	2,974
Dominion	2,148
Imperial	1,415
Crown	1,109
Beaver	1,026
Integrated	600+

- *Register.* Here the lawyers enter the picture. It is crucial for the legal department to ascertain that the name can be registered and protected properly. This requires an audit of all search results, analysis of conflicts, assessment of proprietary components, and documentation of a registration and protection strategy.

Case Example

Akzo: Winning Global Identity

For many years Akzo was a Dutch company that turned out thousands of useful products. Many knew the products, but few knew the company behind them.

Indeed, it was hard to recognize the company because it did business under so many labels. Many of the divisions operated under their own name without acknowledging a relationship to the parent company. There were 10,000 products in over 50 countries being made under a variety of generic and proprietary names.

"Akzo lacked a defined face. We were perceived as pieces, as a blur of business units," says George Arfield, director of Akzo corporate communications. "As a result, if a business unit required a new line of credit, bankers tended to judge it individually, as a small outfit. There was also a negative effect when negotiating acquisitions or joint ventures. Investors did not understand Akzo's true size and scope and acted accordingly."

The lack of a strong global image also hurt when trying to attract desirable candidates for employment. More often than not, potential employees regarded Akzo as a vague coalition of small businesses.

It became evident that Akzo needed a modified approach to business in both form and substance, one that could gain from crystallizing and communicating character, scope, and accomplishments.

In 1985, the company determined that developing a corporate identity had become a critical factor in

- Enhancing the financial world's perception of Akzo.
- Building human resources and creating synergies.
- Developing markets.
- Generating alliances or generating goodwill among publics important to business, clients, employees, communities, and authorities.

Research, performed internally and externally by the British corporate identity consulting firm Wolff Olins, took six months. The external survey was conducted among those influential in the financial, industrial and media sectors in the United Kingdom, France, Sweden, and Germany. The assumption that Akzo was not generally well known was confirmed. Indeed, it was not seen as a company that operated in the vanguard of the chemical industry. Internationally, it was not regarded as a leading European company.

In addition, respondents seemed unaware of many of Akzo's activities. Many had some knowledge of the company, but hardly anyone had the full picture. In some cases, the division names Enka, Sikkens, and Organon were known, but not within the Akzo context. One journalist knew all three names and also knew, more or less, what these companies manufactured; yet he had no idea they were related. As a matter of fact, a trade publication called Akzo "the world's largest unknown chemical company."

The survey revealed that Akzo was perceived as a company that was

- Very Dutch and not too outgoing.
- Rooted in commodity chemicals and synthetic fibers.
- More or less organized as a conglomerate.

Perhaps most damaging in a global context was the fact that Akzo was not rated as a pioneer in high technology. It lagged far behind the profiles presented by rivals such as ICI, Du Pont, BASF, Hoechst, Bayer, and Dow Chemical.

Implementing a Corporate Identity Program. Subsequently, Akzo moved quickly to develop and implement a global corporate identity program that involved the following four phases.

Phase One: Research and Analysis. The first, essential step was to determine what exactly Akzo did stand for. What image did the company want to project? It was decided that Akzo stood for

- Flexibility (the company maintains close contacts with its markets, enabling it to react swiftly to the changing needs of customers)
- Decentralization
- Innovation
- Enterprise
- Alertness
- Responsibility

While leaving the decentralized organizational structure intact, management emphasized the idea of a single enterprise. The message could be summarized as "unity in diversity"—with individual performance viewed as the key to success.

As the business plan progressed, the five divisions—fibers and polymers, salt and basic chemical, chemical, pharmaceutical, and the industrial units of the coatings division, which had been operating under a variety of names—came under a structure that incorporated the parent company's name so that in industrial markets a monolithic identity would be presented. Enka became Akzo Fibers and Polymers, and International Salt was changed to Akzo Salt.

This rather simple (yet novel to the company) decision communicated the unifying spirit. The name Akzo now emerged uniformly and clearly. Every time a division was mentioned, the rest of the company—every other division—gained by association. Brands were retained where necessary.

Phase Two: Development of a New Identity. The next step was creating a new logo to represent the desired qualities. The company believed that the old logo, a triangle, did not reflect the image it wished to project. The question to be answered was, "What identity matches these characteristics?" From the surveys mentioned earlier, one characteristic kept cropping up: a sense of initiative, individuality, and performance among Akzo employees.

Wolff Olins, the company responsible for creating the new symbol for Akzo, was asked to focus on these qualities and add them to other factors as basic themes. Comments Chairman Wally Olins, "It became important to find a symbol that would be beyond class, color, or culture, a symbol that would show the achieving nature of Akzo."

The symbol finally chosen for the company's new image was, ironically, a sculpture dating from 450 B.C., rooted in the culture of ancient Greece. A line drawing of the sculpture was recommended that conveyed these qualities: powerful, worldwide, all-embracing, and future oriented (see Figure 2-1).

Figure 2-1

As this logo was far from neutral, it was decided that an associative survey should be conducted. The new symbol was tested by the Institute for Psychological Market Research, which interviewed both Akzo employees and outside target groups. The plan was to ensure that not too large a gap would be created between the existing and desired corporate image.

Phase Three: Communicating the New Identity. Once the logo was tested and approved, the next step was to introduce it and the global corporate identity it symbolized to senior managers from around the world and to divisional communications departments. This was accomplished at a two-day corporate identity conference in December 1987. Divisional conferences in every country followed.

The new identity was aggressively featured in corporate and divisional employee publications. Business communications vehicles—calling cards, stationery, forms, and checks—were redone in the new scheme. Letters and information kits in seven languages went to clients, suppliers, and financial contacts, while a proactive media-relations campaign got under way.

A comprehensive international corporate ad campaign—the first one ever for the company—was put in place. Full-color ads began running in the business press in the United States, Europe, Asia, and Brazil. Two corporate videos, with soundtracks in major languages, were produced primarily for the worldwide staff. Other projects included totally new corporate and divisional literature, new signs and flags, development of a line of Akzo sportswear for employees, new dinnerware for catering facilities, and a full line of corporate premiums.

Phase Four: Implementation of the New Identity. A comprehensive manual was prepared to help implement the changes and keep the program on track. "It's a living document that is continuously adjusted and updated," explains Arfield. "The manual is the bible of corporate identity, so to speak, and every division or business unit has a person assigned to administer it, in addition to a full-time corporate identity manager at headquarters."

Beyond this, the company began offering professional development programs, as well as total quality courses, all designed to enhance an employee's pride and team spirit.

What have been the results of this ongoing corporate identity project?

"We've learned that reaction to a unified look and symbol is most positive—I guess the military learned that years ago, when they made the word 'uniform' into an adjective and a noun that described not just a garment but an influencer of morale and teamwork," notes Arfield.

As an adjunct to programs that stress quality, human resources development, and R&D, the corporate identity program as an agency of change and progress has been most gratifying.

"If our job as communicators is to satisfy our employers or clients, then we've succeeded," says Arfield. "Our CEO recently said: 'Now when I meet with bankers and other business people in the United States, I seldom have to explain who Akzo is.' "

Case Example

British Telecom: Playing the Name Game

British Telecom, the British firm that has made no secret of its ambition to become a worldwide force in telecommunications, is in the process of changing its name to the more global "BT." The use of initials serves two purposes: It overrides the geographic limitation conveyed by the word "British," and it helps to shake off the firm's image in the United Kingdom as a utility company.

"The name change is a new suit of clothes for us, really," says Bob Raggett, deputy director of corporate relations. "We want to be seen as a world player in the telecommunications field—not as the state-owned monopoly we once were." In short, BT is undergoing a face-lift to reflect the fact that it's a new, caring company—not the old bureaucracy that couldn't care less. It's also out to distance itself from an unhappy history in the mid-1980s, including a storm of complaints about shoddy service after privatization and the bad feelings from a strike in 1987 over employment practices with the engineering staff.

Six years ago, British Telecom underwent privatization. Since then, it has shed over 5,000 U.K. managers to become more streamlined. Today it has staff in over 100 countries that compete for the lucrative MNC market. The company already owns 20 percent of McCaw Cellular Communications, the largest U.S. mobile communications group.

One thing that BT learned from its customers was that they did not want "an overtly British company for their telecommunications needs." Raggett explains: "We find it easier in today's competitive marketplace to have a global identity—or a no-nationality image. We're concentrating on the North American, European, and Pacific Rim markets." He points out that AT&T has employed a similar strategy.

"We realized that you can't put a new image on the same old company—so we've become a new company," says Raggett. With the old symbol and name no longer in synch with the group's international aspirations, a review of both was undertaken with the help of the British identity consulting firm Wolff Olins. The company unveiled its new logo at end-March 1991. The changeover, under the direction of BT Chairman and CEO Iain Vallance, had been accomplished in a little over a year.

According to Vallance, "The old identity was fine for the U.K.-based, state-owned monopoly public utility we were when it was introduced. But it does not match the requirements of a company that must be successful in highly competitive markets worldwide, so that we can grow our business for our shareholders and the people who work in it."

The familiar "T" image has been replaced by a red and blue Pan figure with pipes next to the blue letters "BT." Olins has described it as "a symbol of joyous communication through the ages," designed to set BT apart from the abstract motifs of its international competitors (see logo in Figure 2-2).

Figure 2-2

The symbol is designed to represent the three ideas that are central to the new BT's goal:

- A company that is open and easy to deal with
- A company that is a model among communications companies
- A company with a global future

The redesign project will be extensive: It will involve repainting some 93,000 phone boxes, reprinting stationery, and reconstructing the top of the Telecom Tower in London, still popularly known as the Post Office Tower. Even new staff uniforms are being designed. However, they won't be called uniforms, but rather "image clothing," since they will be donned by many in white-collar management as well as manual laborers. The image overhaul comes with a new advertising slogan for British TV: "You're not just a number."

According to a report in the *Financial Times,* BT's new corporate identity has attracted more than a bit of controversy (although, it notes, not as much as British Petroleum's, now BP, where the police had to be called in at the shareholders' meeting to put down a rumpus when it was revealed that the name change cost £171 million). At a time when layoffs of as many as 36,000 people are expected in the next three years, the £60 million spent to overhaul BT's name and logo is seen by some as unnecessary.

3

Leveraging Brand Equity for Global Competitive Advantage*

Although the corporate name is an essential component in building a global image, it is the product's brand name, along with its "brand equity," that translates directly to business results and profit performance.

By capitalizing on the strength of brands, often a corporation's most valuable asset, global companies can build a formidable arsenal of weapons for competitive insulation. Since 1987, for example, the largest United Kingdom exporter of branded consumer goods, Guinness, has built on its unique position of strength with brand-led business strategies that have leveraged its worldwide distribution to grow earnings per share by 98 percent and dividends per share by 104 percent.

Guinness's United Distillers is now the most profitable international distiller business, and Guinness has moved up to a position second only to Coca-Cola in profits among all the world's beverage companies.

What Drives Brand Equity?

The perception that a customer has of a given brand is a direct reflection of the company's success in managing its investment strategy for all areas of its

---

* This chapter was written by Dunham & Marcus, Inc., International Management Consultants, headquartered in New York City, who are specialists in brand equity management.

business, including marketing, manufacturing, distribution, training, and technology (see Figure 3-1).

The value of brand equity is directly linked to business strategy. As such, what is defined and measured in brand equity must correlate with those factors that are defined and measured in the business strategy (see Table 3-1).

Analyzing Brand Equity

With brand equity directly linked to business strategy, the following drivers of business strategy must be defined as a prerequisite to a brand equity analysis:

- The competitive environment for the business and the competitive set by category, product, and stock-keeping units (SKUs)
- Strategic segments of customers or consumers that drive either volume or profit

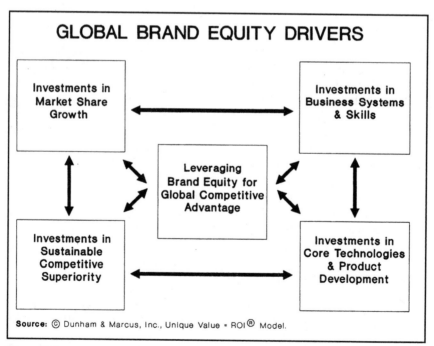

Figure 3-1

Table 3-1. Structure and Definition of a Global Business Strategy*

Component	Primary issue(s) to be addressed
Source of Business/Competitive Framework	Within the identified market/segment, what is the industry structure and global competitive framework? At which competitors' expense does the brand and business source sales and profits?
Market Targets/Key Industry Segments	Within the global market structure, who are the strategic consumer and customer segments that drive near- and long-term sales/profit growth, and whose perception drives brand equity?
Basis for Unique Value® Brand Equity Strategy/Business Superiority	What benefits must be delivered to key strategic segments to sustain perceived competitive superiority? How are existing corporate capabilities/skills leveraged to deliver benefits/services/enhancements that are the basis for global brand equity, market by market?
Product Portfolio Configuration	What is the optimal product portfolio to reinforce the brand's key credentials and deliver the highest returns near and long term?
Profit Drivers	What aspects of brand equity drive profitability and therefore generate the necessary funds for reinvestment in marketing, manufacturing, information systems, and core technologies? Where can global economies of scale be leveraged?
Key Factors for Success	What factors drive successful implementation globally and locally?

* © Dunham & Marcus, Inc., 1981.

- The functional and emotional benefits that are generic to the category and the key benefits that provide the basis for differentiation from competitors
- The products, SKUs, and product attributes that support and deliver the key benefits
- The factors that drive profitability

After this analysis is completed, there are integrated elements of brand equity that must be defined and measured. These include the brand's

- Perceived added value and uniqueness versus its competitors

- Presence in the marketplace in terms of effective distribution (numbers of consumers or customers it reaches, and how often)

- Basis for perceived quality (a function of intangibles such as imagery, as well as tangibles such as manufacturing standards and specifications)

- Price value (perceived value in conjunction with business system efficiencies)

- Service support credentials (a reflection of corporate training strategies and practices)

- Overall stature as a category leader, which is related to investments in continuous improvements, product and service innovation, R&D programs, and management vision

Dunham & Marcus's proprietary Unique Value = ROI® business model (see p. 35 for an in-depth discussion) measures the fundamentals of business strategy as outlined above. This analysis crystallizes the key factors for return on investment (ROI) and the role of brand equity in managing a business for superior profit performance. It also permits a company to focus on those substrategies for brand equity that are needed to focus investment resources by corporate function, such as marketing, manufacturing, and research and development (R&D) to prioritize investments in building brands.

Brand Equity Drivers

Other factors contributing to the brand and the potential for building equity that should be analyzed by the company include the brand's set of associations, its perceived quality, and the proprietary brand assets and technologies.

The Brand's Set of Associations. Brand associations are measurable benefits and attributes assigned to the brand by customers and consumers. These may reflect physical product features; emotional attitudes about the life-styles, values, and behavior of the people who use the brand or the moods; and occasions associated with the use of the brand. These associations must be specific and measurable to drive management's investment decisions in manufacturing, information systems, training, and technology.

When brand associations are highly relevant to the needs or aspirations of a consumer segment or, in industrial or business-to-business categories, a customer segment, higher pricing and margins are justified. Image Leverage® (see p. 46) opportunities can also be developed cost efficiently to broaden the brand's portfolio of businesses, as in the case of IBM's personal computers and Vaseline Intensive Care Hand Lotion (see the following IBM and Vaseline case examples).

Case Example

IBM: Managing Brand Equity Globally

IBM's history and initials once stood for unapproachable, technical International Business Machines. Its goal today is to modify any residual, perceived unfriendliness or arrogance and be known as a highly responsive service supplier to a full array of constituencies. As a result, in the past 10 years, IBM has recognized the need to develop global brand equity strategies that are separate from its corporate image.

IBM's challenge is to develop a strategy to establish its brand equity as relevant and superior for a broad spectrum of branded, global products and services ranging from consumer-focused, personal systems to the most sophisticated mainframes.

The drivers behind IBM's global strategy development are the universal perceptions of IBM, says Byron Quann, director of marketing services. "Even though we don't have a direct program to manage brand equity globally," he says, "we are out in five to six countries a year looking at IBM's image with a variety of parameters, among a wide range of constituencies—from customers to employees to government officials. As you start to look at the various geographies and the various constituencies, you don't see a lot of difference."

IBM is using mass communication channels to advertise aggressively in order to build its global brand equity. Critical to this communication is delivering the overall message of IBM's commitment to customer satisfaction in a way that is relevant for each line of business and product. "With enterprise systems [mainframes], you clearly do have critical, 24-hour operations with all of the expectations of traditional IBM service," says Charles Pankenier, director of communications operation. "At the other end of the marketplace, you need to figure out some other way to deliver the service content to a consumer of a personal system. At the same time, you must get them conditioned to the fact that it does not necessarily mean that some IBM person is going to show up at their door if they have a problem later."

Quann summarizes IBM's position on consistent global strategy development. "We are anticipating the world shrinking; increased cross-border shopping, the result of what is going to happen with the European Community in 1992. There is great likelihood that IBM will be increasingly perceived as a whole as opposed to being unique in each constituency. It is a good idea, therefore, to understand that perception in a global sense."

Case Example

Leveraging the Vaseline Brand

In 1970, Chesebrough-Pond's leveraged the Vaseline name and its strong associations onto a new product in the hand and body lotion category. By leveraging Vaseline's unique brand equity and positioning the product as a therapeutic healing agent rather than a cosmetic lotion, Chesebrough-Pond's quickly established Vaseline Intensive Care as a leader in a market that was new to the corporation. Within a year, Vaseline Intensive Care had captured the number one market position, overtaking longtime leader Jergens for dominance of the category.

In 1987, Unilever purchased Chesebrough-Pond's to strengthen its worldwide position in health and beauty care, clearly recognizing the value of the Vaseline and Vaseline Intensive Care brand equities. Using a concept first successful in Australia, in 1988 Vaseline Intensive Care Hand and Nail lotion was launched in world markets and is now a significant contributor to the Vaseline Intensive Care business. Similarly, Unilever Japan's development of a Vaseline Intensive Care line extension with a mild everyday sun screen was so successful that it is now being introduced globally. The strategy is to roll out every successful country initiative for Vaseline Intensive Care globally, reinforcing brand equity from the bottom up, while top management ensures strategic continuity and consistency.

Perceived Quality.   The tangible value in a product or service is not necessarily the same as the perceived value of its performance, reliability, and consistency. Perceptions can be either better or worse than reality. Generally, the higher the perceived quality, the greater the product's value and the more customers are willing to pay, especially in prestige categories where the brand is a status symbol, such as Rolls-Royce, Mercedes, and BMW cars. The reverse is also true, as in the case of Cadillac (see General Motors-Cadillac case example p. 36).

Proprietary Brand Assets and Technologies.   The most tangible aspects of brand equity are exclusive or ownable assets such as patents, licenses, trademarks, and logos. For example, while Johnson & Johnson (J&J) built the Tylenol brand on the basis of a patent, J&J's consistent investment in branding has transcended the life of the patent.

Developing a Brand Equity Strategy

The process for leveraging brand equity for global competitive advantage begins by determining the specific attributes that set a company's brand apart from the competition in a way that is most relevant to the needs of the market. This analysis must be rigorously conducted if it is to optimize the opportunity to manage brand equity strategically for superior and sustainable profit performance.

The Unique Value = ROI® model identifies the key factors in a business analysis that must be understood, interrelated, and measured to determine the strategy that maximizes the added value of brand equity. Initially, the model is a conceptual analytical framework. A computer model is then built to support management decision making for key investments in brand equity (see Figure 3-2).

The model in the chart provides the framework for identifying the Unique Value® factors such as:

1. The key customer and consumer benefits and segments that drive the size and loyalty patterns of the core franchise

2. The key manufacturing and delivery systems needed to meet expectations and satisfy demand cost efficiently, such as continuous quality improvement programs and just-in-time delivery systems

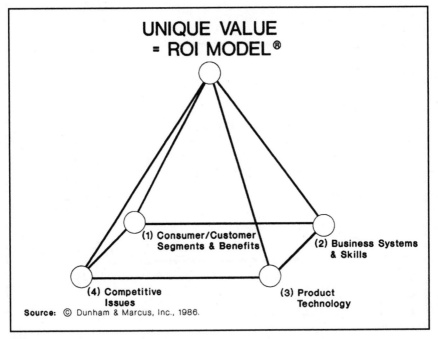

Figure 3-2

3. The optimal product line to deliver the key benefits and to compete cost effectively in the maximum number of occasions

4. The strengths and weaknesses of direct competitors by purchase occasion

The preceding four analyses are performed iteratively to identify the Unique Value® factors critical to managing brand equity for global competitive advantage (see Figure 3-3).

Case Example

General Motors: No Longer the "Cadillac"

At one time, the "Cadillac" of any category was synonymous with the gold standard by which all others were judged. But in the last 10 years, a dramatic reversal has displaced Cadillac from its position and significantly eroded the value and relevance of its name and its brand equity (see Figure 3-4).

Cadillac's declining market share is linked directly to General Motors' failure to invest in the luxury car segment in order to remain

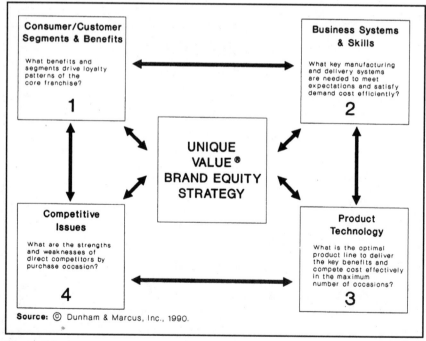

Source: © Dunham & Marcus, Inc., 1990.

Figure 3-3

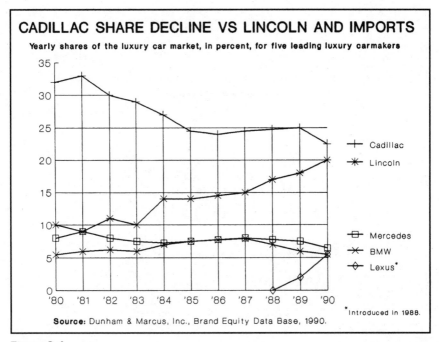

CADILLAC SHARE DECLINE VS LINCOLN AND IMPORTS

Yearly shares of the luxury car market, in percent, for five leading luxury carmakers

*Introduced in 1988.

Source: Dunham & Marcus, Inc., Brand Equity Data Base, 1990.

Figure 3-4

competitive with European standards of quality and luxury and meet the changing needs of the American luxury car buyer (see Figure 3-5).

During the 1970s, a new car market emerged, the contemporary luxury segment. U.S. manufacturers, including Cadillac, made no attempt to establish a presence. This segment was built by Mercedes and BMW, whose combined sales grew from 104,820 units in 1981 to 198,628 units in 1986, while Cadillac's sales declined, according to *Automotive News*.

Cadillac compounded its loss of leadership and relevance by addressing the wrong set of issues in its design of the Cimarron. This new car was introduced in the United States in 1981, with a smaller chassis and what was perceived to be an underpowered engine. Loyal Cadillac owners and U.S. buyers of imported luxury cars reacted with extreme disappointment to the U.S. automobile industry for its lack of market understanding and responsiveness (see Figure 3-6). As a result, even within its own segment, the traditional U.S. luxury car market, Cadillac sales fell sharply relative to Ford's Lincoln, its primary competitor. While the Cimarron was a product failure, the damaging impact on Cadillac's long-term brand equity was much more costly. During the last few years, however, General Motors has reappraised its

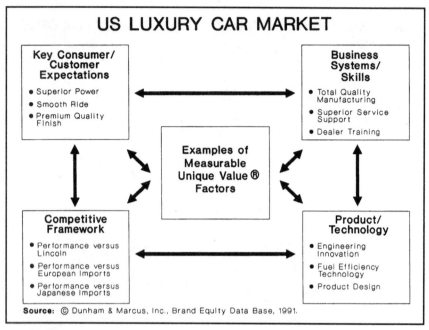

Figure 3-5

management of the Cadillac business and is in the process of a long-term reinvestment program. One positive result was Cadillac's success last year in winning the prestigious Malcolm Baldrige National Quality Award.

Measuring and Managing Brand Equity Strategy

Measuring key factors for brand equity gauges the return on all investments in the brand. Thus, building brand equity requires continuous tracking of not only advertising and promotion, but also manufacturing, distribution, training, quality improvements, innovations in product, packaging, and communications, and all other forms of brand franchise enhancement.

When a brand-driven global business strategy is in place, it addresses in a fully integrated way the questions in Table 3-1.

The Brand Equity Substrategies

Developing and implementing long-term strategies for building and managing brands also requires a series of substrategies, including executional guidelines that ensure perceived uniformity of product quality and service

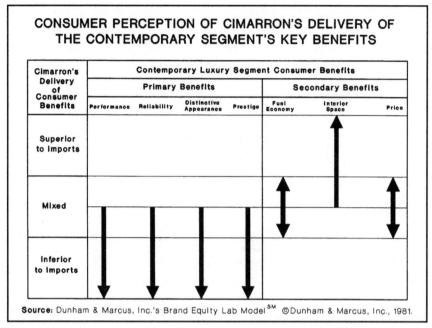

CONSUMER PERCEPTION OF CIMARRON'S DELIVERY OF THE CONTEMPORARY SEGMENT'S KEY BENEFITS

Source: Dunham & Marcus, Inc.'s Brand Equity Lab Model[SM] ©Dunham & Marcus, Inc., 1981.

Figure 3-6

support at every customer interface. The four global substrategies that must be managed are (1) marketing, (2) manufacturing and distribution, (3) product and technology, and (4) competitive strategies (see Figure 3-7).

Global Marketing Strategies.   In analyzing global marketing strategies there are several components that companies must examine. These include strategic segmentation, advertising, and a consistent brand name and logo policy:

- *Strategic segmentation.* Although cultural differences exist between regions and markets, global corporations increasingly find similarities in terms of values, life-styles, aspirations, and physical and emotional needs. For example, the U.S.-headquartered greeting card company Hallmark has found that many of its card lines have appeal all over the world. Similarly, when U.S.-based publisher *Reader's Digest* tests book titles globally, it also finds that the top two or three titles have universal popularity across countries and nationalities.

- *Advertising.* Advertising expenditures are an indicator of the economics of brand equity. In the United States alone, annual advertising

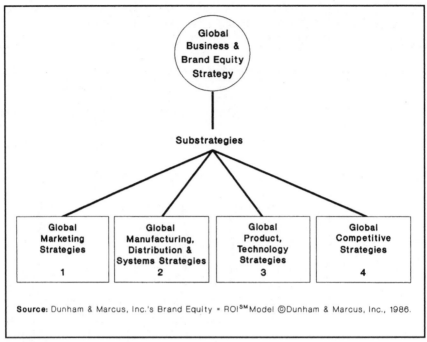

Source: Dunham & Marcus, Inc.'s Brand Equity = ROI^SM Model ©Dunham & Marcus, Inc., 1986.

Figure 3-7

expenditures totaled $136 billion in 1990. Advertising analysts project annual expenditures to reach $3 trillion worldwide by the end of the decade.

Successful management of the marketing strategy for building equity is more complex when the brand name and corporate name are the same as, for instance, with IBM (see case example p. 33), Mitsubishi, Sony, American Express, Du Pont, and Chevron. Dr. Lewis C. Winters, manager of research, public affairs, at Chevron Corp., believes that investments in the brand benefit both the corporation and its image: "Increased marketing activity and, specifically, brand advertising has accelerated the improvement in attitudes toward oil companies. For the most part we have found that marketing is the essential corporate communications tool." This is especially true in Japan, where strong corporate credentials heavily influence consumer purchase decisions.

Although global advertising development is normally driven by a single, comprehensive worldwide strategy, local implementation is often varied. For instance, while American Express centralizes its marketing function, it uses carefully managed, local executions of campaign concepts. American Express defines "prestige," "service," and "security" as the fundamental benefits uniquely associated with its brand. In its advertising campaigns, these benefits are communicated in the form of campaign themes such as "Membership has its privileges" and "Don't leave home without it," which are translated and used worldwide. Executional differences include casting and locations.

- *Consistent brand name and logo.*   Global brands use the same name and logo design wherever they are distributed. The result is increased consumer recognition and consistent brand name associations worldwide. "It gives the buyer comfort," says Richard A. Russack, managing director of the public relations firm Adams & Rinehart, who handles public relations for Joseph E. Seagram and Sons Inc.

    "The more consumers travel," says Russack, "the more comfort they will find in a familiar brand name. It assures them of product quality and consistency, whether they are in Brussels or Bangkok."

Global Manufacturing, Distribution, and Systems Strategies

- *Manufacturing.*   Increasingly, global marketers are investing in manufacturing technology that can meet high standards of consistency with tight specifications across markets. More sophisticated consumer expectations, driven by cross-border shopping, make it imperative that products meet the same quality standard throughout the world.

    Nevertheless, few companies expressly link production strategy to brand equity. Production facilities that are faster and cheaper can reinforce the equities of brands by delivering superior benefits and value to customers more cost efficiently.

    For example, by manufacturing branded goods in countries where labor costs are low, a business enhances value-added branded profit margins with low-cost producer status. Corporations such as Electrolux, General Electric, Mitsubishi, Sony, Toyota, and Unilever leverage increasing economies of scale by investing in state-of-the-art manufacturing and information technologies at fewer but more efficient locations. Mitsubishi makes compressors for air conditioners in Thailand, elevators for the Chinese market through a joint venture in Shanghai, auto parts in Illinois, projection televisions in southern California, and VCRs in Scotland.

    In the auto industry, the concept of "lean production," originated by the Toyota Motor Co. in Japan, is now spreading to North America and Western Europe. *The Machine That Changed the World,* by James P. Womack, Daniel T. Jones, and Daniel Roos, shows that lean production welds the activities of everyone, from top management to line workers to suppliers, into a tightly integrated whole that can respond almost instantly to marketing demands from consumers, to reinforce the relevance, value, and competitive superiority of branded products.

- *Distribution.*   It is also critical to manage distribution systems in a way that is consistent with and enhances brand equity. For instance, the German consumer electronics manufacturer Braun has a distribution strategy for top-of-the-line coffee makers, which sell through upscale department stores such as Bloomingdale's in the United States and Harrod's in the United Kingdom, while its lower-end models are distributed through stores such as K Mart in the United States.

- *Information systems.*   Linked to distribution strategy, information systems enhance global brand equity by going well beyond sales information and inventory control. Strategic decision support systems can tie information technology to continuous tracking studies that answer questions about the brand and its user base in relation to advertising, promotion, pricing activity, and competitive initiatives. For example, using the input from 10,000 hand-held computers, PepsiCo's Frito-Lay transmits daily product movement information overnight in the United States to the company's information network. Data are accessible to top management by the next day. In using inventory control to reinforce brand equity, the system includes product freshness information, which speeds the removal of stale products from the shelf and reinforces Frito-Lay's key brand benefits of "freshness" and "crunchiness," critical for consumer satisfaction and loyalty. With its Frito-Lay U.S. system fully operational, PepsiCo Foods International is poised to leverage similar information technology to support its growing global snack food operations.

  American Airlines also pioneered the brand-driven use of information technology to reward loyal customers with its frequent-flier program and reinforce brand equity. Following privatization, British Airways has managed frequent-flier reward programs driven by information technology to support its claim to be "the world's favorite airline."

Product and Technology Strategies

- *Product Technology.*   Procter & Gamble's (P&G's) philosophy of building brands and brand equities is to invest consistently and aggressively in marketing and technology programs to gain the greatest return from long-term brand building. Now sold in 78 countries, Pampers diapers is a global P&G brand that has received a rapid transfer of technology and strong advertising support worldwide. The expansion of Pampers to Ultra-Pampers (using its thin diaper technology) and the recent boy/girl

Pampers introduction in 20 countries are a result of P&G's global planning process for its diaper business. "I see no reason why we shouldn't expect our global share of our major core categories to grow at least another 10 points, to 25 percent of the market during the '90s," Edwin Artzt, chairman and CEO of P&G, told a group of financial analysts last May.

- *Packaging.* Standardized packaging is critical to a cross-border presence in the global marketplace. As consumers begin to shop across borders more frequently, uniform packaging is the basis for immediate acceptance. Recognition as the same brand anywhere in the world is part of the prestige of world-class brand equity. If travelers want a Pepsi or a bottle of Johnny Walker Scotch, they can find the familiar can or bottle. The universal availability provides a strong reinforcement of the brand's worldwide and world-class status.

Global Competitive Strategies.   Acquiring strong global brand equities can significantly enhance a company's competitive position. When the U.K.'s Bass PLC purchased the U.S.-headquartered Holiday Inn hotel chain, it became the leading player in the international lodging industry. At that time, Holiday Inn had 1600 hotels in 48 countries.

According to Ian Prosser, chairman of Bass, the underleveraged strength of the Holiday Inn brand name will drive competitive strategies as Bass expands Holiday Inn internationally by building new hotels and targeting smaller hotel chains as a main source of business.

Bass will invest $1 billion in its global hotel business over the next three years, adding 50,000 rooms and upgrading product quality and standards. Key geographic areas of development include the United Kingdom, where more than 30 additional hotels will be built by 1995, and Asia/Pacific, where 27 hotels are currently under construction.

Benefits of Brand Equity

There are several crucial benefits that a company can expect from developing a focused brand equity strategy. These include enhanced profitability, reduced product introduction cost, ability to set a premium price, and increased name recognition.

Profit Performance

When managed successfully, brand equity is a driver of market share and, therefore, profitability. Studies based on PIMS' (Profit Impact of Market

Strategy) data base of 2600 businesses show that, on average, products with a market share of 40 percent generated three times the ROI of those with a market share of only 10 percent.

A United Kingdom study of grocery brands shows that the number one brand generates more than six times the return on sales of the number two brand, while the number three and four brands are unprofitable (see Figure 3-8).

Investment in brand share building programs can therefore accelerate returns significantly, while long-term ROI is positively affected by margin expansion made possible by leveraging fixed and direct costs to achieve volume growth and price leadership (the ability to lead a category price increase as a result of a dominant market position with consumers and distributors).

Reduced Introduction Costs

For global corporations that have developed portfolios of strong brand equities, leveraging brand equity into new business opportunities is often the most cost-effective and profitable growth opportunity from an investment perspective. The cost of launching a major new brand in the late 1980s was at least $100 million in the United States alone. Success for new

Market Share Rank and Average Net Margins for UK Grocery Brands

Rank	Net Margin (%)
1	17.9
2	2.8
3	-0.9
4	-5.9

Source: PIMS Data.

Figure 3-8

branded businesses was estimated at only 15–20 percent, according to the Marketing Science Institute, a United States leader in business research.

If planned carefully and executed strategically, a new product can both leverage and build a parent brand and the core business. In the United States, examples of new consumer products that have accomplished this dual goal are Maxwell House Masterblend Coffee and Duncan Hines Microwave Duncan's Cups.

Premium Pricing

An important advantage for global brands is their ability to command premium pricing. In competition with a global brand, local brands, lacking economies of scale as well as resources, are at a significant cost and pricing disadvantage. Costs are higher, resources are fewer, and the temptation is to resort to price-reduction tactics, which reinforce a perceived lack of quality. In markets around the world, Coke and Pepsi maintain a price premium compared with local colas, but both are growing at the expense of local colas because of the global brands' perceived superiority.

Increased Name Recognition

Business strategy legitimately looks for opportunities to leverage corporate assets. In the case of brand names, the assets are intangible, but powerful. Canon leveraged its name and reputation for high-quality photography and lens equipment into Canon copier machines; Chanel brought its upscale fashion name to the fragrance business; Rossignol used its brand equity and credentials for high-quality skis to enter the ski boot business. Each of these brand names brought not only high name recognition to its targeted category, but also instant credibility with key constituencies.

At present, Sony is leveraging its credentials to penetrate a challenging new market. The company, in an attempt to leverage its name into medical electronics, has begun marketing two new video systems to hospitals. Sony's entry into the medical electronics business is an effort to rejuvenate its mature video technologies. Analysts are confident that Sony will be successful and that the Sony brand name will be an important factor in this success.

The introduction of AT&T's new credit card, the *Universal Card,* further illustrates this strategy. Commenting on the new card, Robert Allen, the company's CEO, told the Conference Board, "positive values transfer into other markets and other venues. AT&T entered the credit card business in 1990 with a product called the AT&T Universal Card. The company had no track record in this market and zero customer base—only the value of the

AT&T brand name. Seven months after the launch, the AT&T Universal Card cracked the top-five list of American credit cards. More than five million people now hold this card."

Globalizing Brand Equity

Historically, U.S. corporations have been far less global in their vision than corporations headquartered in regions that must export, such as Japan and Europe. Outstanding exceptions do exist, such as American Express, whose global presence is driven by its travel-related business.

One of the barriers to developing a global strategy today is the corporation's organizational structure and culture. A long organizational history of decentralization may create some reluctance to impose centrally managed standards for brand equity, especially for more recently acquired businesses. To succeed, the corporation must manage a complex set of internal communication mechanisms to overcome organizational barriers to global uniformity, as Unilever does in its constant sharing of ideas, successes, and "best practice" experiences across national boundaries.

Leveraging Brand Equity Globally

Dunham & Marcus uses Image Leverage® models to look at brand equity in the context of portfolio optimization. Strategies define how the parent brand can become an umbrella and span a broader range of products or businesses to optimize economies of scale or move into more profitable business areas. Strong brand equity cannot automatically be leveraged into a new product or new business.

To leverage a brand successfully requires careful attention to Image Leverage® principles, consistent with the fundamentals of business strategy. The company must put in place a program to evaluate brand credentials, qualify the customer base, evaluate perceptions, and get top management support.

Evaluate Brand Credentials.   Leveraging brand equity requires brand credentials that are perceived to be not only relevant but superior to competitors in the context of the targeted business.

Specific questions to be asked include the following:

1. Are the brand credentials valuable in the context of the new category and superior to existing competitors?

2. Does the brand carry negative associations in the new context?

3. Will the use of the brand name in a new category reinforce or be consistent with its current equity? Will it put the brand's current equity at risk?

4. Will the resulting portfolio of businesses and products be more valuable to the corporation over the long term?

5. If successful, does the corporation have the resources to sustain the investment until it is established and profitable?

Qualify the Customer Base. According to Allen Rosenshine, chairman of the advertising agency BBDO, leveraging a brand name can backfire. Gillette in the United States "decided it was going to market a female-oriented antiperspirant deodorant. Obviously, empirical evidence suggests that you would not put the Gillette name on a female deodorant, since that is not what the Gillette megabrand represents," he says.

In the absence of a prelaunch analysis, subsequent experience confirmed that the Gillette name, linked with strong masculine imagery, did not have the associations women were looking for in a personal hygiene product. Furthermore, the introduction of a product for women also had serious risks for Gillette's male consumer franchise.

Evaluate Perceptions

Global brand equity is generally regarded as problematic where food is concerned, because tastes are an expression of culture. Unilever does not attempt to cross borders with basic foods, such as soup, citing examples like extreme cultural disparities between Dutch and French concepts of pea soup. And whereas tea drinking is a cultural ritual in both Japan and the United Kingdom, its meaning and practice are very different in each country.

On the other hand, if the values inherent in brand equity relate to a more broadly defined experience rather than a narrowly defined product, cultural differences are not a constraint. American fast-food chains such as McDonald's and Pizza Hut have demonstrated that an eating experience can be branded in such a way that regional differences can be transcended.

Get Top Management Support

BBDO's Rosenshine sums up the realities of rising to the challenge of managing brand equity globally: "In the end, I find it hard to imagine an argument against globalization under the right marketing circumstances. However, the execution of it will be measured in direct proportion to the management commitment. While globalization is inevitable, it will require significant leadership to make it happen within a reasonable time frame."

In Dunham & Marcus's experience, world-class companies are already dealing with the need for global brands in the face of increasing global competition. The investments in market share growth, total quality manufacturing, information technology, training, and product development that corporations such as Bass, Du Pont, Sony, and Unilever are making are all in support of the formidable economic and competitive leverage that global brand equity represents.

Case Example

Du Pont: Managing Global Brand Equity

The U.S.-based chemical company E.I. Du Pont de Nemours has developed a two-pronged brand equity strategy. It is incorporating brand equity management in its business, and, importantly, it is also linking certain established brands to the corporate name to enhance the global presence of the Du Pont brand.

Du Pont defines its overall corporate image as a complex set of factors, over many of which it has little control (see Figure 3-9).

By contrast, its brand equity can be controlled by a consistent and purposeful investment in the strategically important values inherent in the name. Du Pont's brand equity strategy is to build its corporate name into a unique asset with a role to play in supporting its worldwide businesses for competitive advantage.

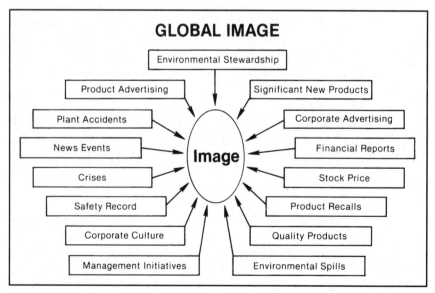

Figure 3-9

Lee Tashjian, vice president of public affairs, explains that the purpose of Du Pont's current corporate "image" advertising is to "create a value-added dimension to the Du Pont corporate name. This allows Du Pont to more strongly associate brand names with our corporate identity, providing us with extra marketing leverage that is difficult for our principal competitors to generate."

In targeted European countries, the corporate name is being managed in concert with leading consumer-product-focused brands. Du Pont's Lycra, for example, has strong brand equity in the apparel market. Recognizing this, the company recently conducted a study in the United Kingdom and Italy to determine the potential for enhancing its corporate image by strengthening the association between the Lycra brand name and Du Pont.

As a result of the study's findings, management plans to link the Lycra name with Du Pont in global markets. By associating with Lycra, a well-established, high-investment brand equity with recognition as a premium quality, contemporary product that meets consumers' needs, Du Pont can reinforce its corporate objective of being recognized as a company that delivers innovative and superior products that satisfy customer and consumer needs, and disassociate its credentials from the unpredictable fortunes of the chemical industry.

In the United States, Du Pont's brand equity and corporate image-building strategies are helping to improve the company's favorability rating. Du Pont has successfully distanced itself from its industry, and is now seen as a highly value-added manufacturer of differentiated products and services that justify significant price premiums (see Figure 3-10).

Du Pont also is focusing its worldwide image and brand-building efforts in Japan, where corporate image is important to consumer brand preference. In Japan, being perceived as a "first-class" company is critical to product acceptance and drives purchase behavior. For Du Pont's annual "Corporate Image Study," an independent Tokyo research firm tracks customer perceptions of more than 35 companies, including Du Pont. Through this research, Du Pont has learned that to have a strong corporate image in Japan requires at least 50 percent of respondents, when asked to describe a company, to select "first class" from a list of more than 20 image attributes, including "trustworthy," "stable," and "has tradition." By using precisely targeted advertising, Du Pont has increased its "first class" rating by more than 50 percent, from 21 percent in 1984 to 32.5 percent in 1989. This is well on the way to meeting the company's objective of 54 percent by 1994, close to IBM's current rating of 57 percent (see Figure 3-11).

Additional Reference Material

"Brand Extensions. The Good, Bad, and the Ugly," David Aaker, *Sloan Management Review*, Summer 1990.

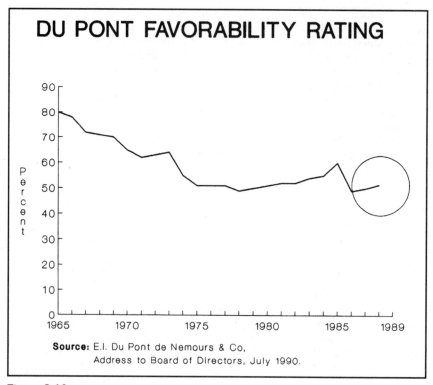

Figure 3-10

Market Driven Strategy: Processes for Creative Value, George S. Day, Free Press, 1990.

"Segmentation and ROI: How Precise Segmentation Impacts Profit Performance," Andrea Dunham, Address to the Conference Board 1990 Marketing Conference.

A Force for Change: How Leadership Differs From Management, John P. Kotter, Free Press, 1990.

The Measurements and Determinants of Brand Equity: A Financial Approach, Carol J. Simon and Mary W. Sullivan, University of Chicago Press, 1990.

Managing Across Borders, Christopher A. Bartlett and Sumantra Ghoshal, Harvard Business School Press, 1989.

Accounting for Brands, Patrick Barwise, Christopher Higson, Andrew Likierman, and Paul Marsh, London Business School, 1989.

Defining, Measuring and Managing Brand Equity, Lance Leuthesser, Marketing Science Institute, 1988.

"Does It Pay To Advertise to Hostile Audiences With Corporate Advertising," Dr. Lewis C. Winters, *Journal of Advertising Research,* June/July 1988.

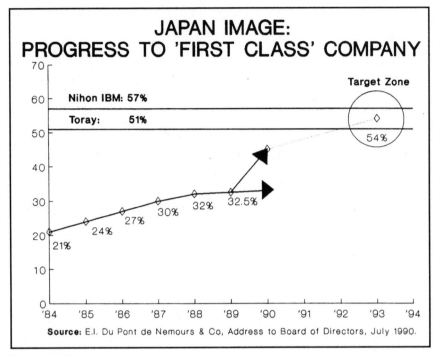

Figure 3-11

Creating Shareholder Value: The New Standard for Business Performance, Alfred Rappaport, Free Press, 1986.

"The Effect of Brand Advertising on Company Image: Implications for Corporate Advertising," Dr. Lewis C. Winters, *Journal of Advertising Research,* April/May 1986.

"New Product Marketing in an Era of Transition," Andrea Dunham, Address to the American Marketing Association New Products Conference, New York, June 14, 1983.

4

How to Build
a Global Image

In an increasingly competitive marketplace, establishing and presenting a global image can provide a resource for building understanding, credibility, and support among a variety of key "publics." An image campaign went a long way in establishing a worldwide corporate and brand name for both Reebok and Apple Computer.

Developing an Image Strategy

What is the best way to build a global image? The first step is to determine your corporate identity. This is mainly an open-ended, investigative, analytical process, usually involving experienced identity consultants who will probe the company, its industry, the marketplace, and the competitive environment to determine how best to position and project the organization for the near- and the longer-term future.

The process includes a careful review of all available research, reports, and studies along with a range of communication materials on the company and industry.

In addition, a series of confidential interviews is conducted with a representative sampling of internal and external audiences—from senior executives to board members to middle management to rank-and-file employees; and from security analysts to suppliers to customers to competitors. The goal is to get a broad cross section of opinion about the organization and its business environment.

What is the benefit of all this strategic soul searching? By determining its special style, quality, and character, a company is better able to position itself in its marketplaces and to differentiate its capabilities against the competition with greater precision, clarity, and impact. Only when the company determines what it really stands for can a focus and commitment be projected.

The Image Process

According to Clive Chajet, chairman and CEO of Lippincott & Margulies, there are several steps that companies can take to achieve a global image.

- Assess the fundamental identity and image management practices of your corporation from an international perspective.

- Develop a global mission statement that crystallizes your business intent, scope, and strategy for both your current market as well as those you plan to seek in the future.

- Create a positioning document of the company's basic beliefs, credo, and values; its areas of business concentration; strategy for growth; commitment to research and development; geographic reach, as well as its desired image; and the tone and manner for all communications—whether "passportless," local in flavor, or particularly nationalistic.

- Develop a naming system that encompasses not only the corporate name, but the business's operating entities, products, and services. Do the rules that guide your naming practices in the United States apply to the European market? The Japanese market? Is there a mechanism to facilitate the development of future names and ensure that they meet the criteria established to reinforce overall international product goals?

- Create a graphic design system that establishes and institutionalizes a uniform representation of the company and its quality standards in the development of all communications, ranging from corporate and product collateral to facilities, signage, trucks, and uniforms. Do the rules that guide your graphic design system accommodate the varied styles, tastes, and cultural idiosyncrasies of the other countries where you operate?

- Set priorities for external communications practices and policies.

- Articulate clearly the appropriate roles for advertising, public relations, sales promotion, community relations, and development to ensure that such communications meet the guidelines for reinforcing a desired image on the corporate or product level.

The Mission Statement

Companies will find the corporate mission statement extremely important in conveying a global image. Such a declaration is even more essential for the decentralized or diversified company. The statement helps the company position itself with those outside the company and cements a global corporate culture within.

The following are some of the benefits that result from stating a corporate mission:

1. Top management will have a central force that motivates the company and its employees. It can then adapt existing cultures with greater sensitivity and integrate new cultures, following a merger and/or acquisition (M&A), with less turmoil.

2. Strategic planners can zero in on the basic values, beliefs, and motivations in selecting M&A candidates that will fit well from a corporate culture standpoint. This could prevent the mixing of one company's oil with another's water.

3. Marketing managers will receive clear signals on how best to convey corporate culture across the range of divisions and products. Corporate reputation is enhanced by such uniformity.

4. Public and investor relations professionals will have a clearly defined and internally consistent company line. A platform will be provided for solid corporate advertising. These communications efforts build upon and reinforce each other's focused messages.

5. Human resources managers and recruitment personnel can better understand the kinds of employees who would flourish—or flounder—in their company's particular environment. Such an appreciation can attract needed talent and avoid costly hiring mistakes. Moreover, current employees will show greater pride in an organization whose purpose and direction they more clearly comprehend.

Who Influences the Strategy?

In building a global image, interaction with many "publics" must be taken into account. While every company must develop its own unique approach, Brouillard Communications, a division of J. Walter Thompson, suggests the following groups be kept in mind when developing a global image strategy:

- *The financial community.* For many companies, this is the most important public. It includes financial analysts in addition to other financial professionals, such as investment bankers, underwriters, brokers, mutual fund and institutional portfolio managers, and trust officers. Also included are the financial press and potential investors, whether institutional or individual.

- *The business community.* Customers, suppliers, and competitors fall into this category, as do other companies that may be candidates for acquisitions, mergers, and joint ventures. These make up the "peer group," which judges, criticizes, and, at the same time, does business with a company.

- *Consumers.* Consumers are increasingly demanding that corporations be more than providers of goods and services. They want companies to "stand for something." After the freewheeling 1980s, many customers are asking that the companies with which they do business evidence concern not only for product quality, but also for the impact their business has on the quality of life in their country, community, and the world marketplace.

- *Other "thought" leaders.* These are individuals from the media, universities, civic organizations, and the religious community who exert influence over public opinion.

- *The corporate team.* An all-important public in a successful corporate communications program are the members of a company's own corporate team: its top managers, employees, and current shareholders. As they are the ones who will be called upon to describe and explain the corporate culture, they need assistance and direction.

- *Government.* In every country in which a company conducts business, it is imperative that the government be kept apprised of corporate intentions and requirements.

Case Example

Reebok: Extending an Image

Market research indicated that Reebok International Ltd., an established $1.5-billion corporation with a short, eight-year history, needed an expanded corporate identity—a cohesive, global identity that could be channeled to energize its maturing brands. "Cool," "trendy," and "vibrant"—words frequently used to describe the company—had been replaced with "comfortable," "standard," and "middle class."

The challenge for Reebok was to make its mainstream marketing position exciting. As fierce competitors LA Gear and Nike were firmly developing new marketing strategies, the company also needed to stand for something beyond its product—to find a strategic platform that was uniquely the property of Reebok.

"More and more in the marketplace, it is our feeling that who you are and what you stand for are as important as the quality of the product you sell," says Ken Lightcap, vice president of corporate communications for the Stoughton, Massachusetts-based footwear manufacturer. "Keds, Adidas, Nike all offer similar products. What we wanted to do was establish our image so firmly that when people all over the world bought our product, they knew who they were buying it from." Furthermore, rising worldwide sales demanded that this new image extend well internationally to solidify Reebok's position as a global marketer.

The Issue-Related Image.   Reebok decided its image should be related to a particular concern of young people the world over. (Research indicated that high school and college students—deemed essential to the energy of the brand—were becoming interested in cause-related issues.) The issue chosen was human rights, a basic global concern that dovetailed well with the existing corporate philosophy advocating freedom of expression.

Says CEO Paul Fireman, "I wanted to put together a business that would make a difference. I wanted to have something to do that would make me feel good inside. I wanted a business where freedom of expression was a way of life."

"We did not want our image to be something that we were not," continues Lightcap. "We wanted to recognize freedom of expression around the world, just as it is recognized within the company. This is a vision, an attitude, that permeates all Reebok employees, who are encouraged to speak out, be creative. The Reebok culture speaks to the entrepreneur, for that's who started this company. We aren't heavily into corporate training programs. What we like are 'pockets of thought.' Differences are encouraged among Reebok employees. I guess the corporate image we were trying to establish was a natural fallout of the way the company perceives itself—as making a difference worldwide."

To tie itself strategically to the human rights issue, Reebok decided to underwrite Amnesty International's "Human Rights Now!" world concert tour. Requesting that it be the only sponsor, in return, Reebok asked that "Made possible by the Reebok Foundation" be placed on programs and concert publicity. The tour, which began in 1988, was designed to raise awareness of human rights issues through a series of rock concerts.

As the underwriter, Reebok had an interesting yet challenging role: a corporate leader that was now a partner of Amnesty International, a worldwide nonprofit organization that promotes the cause of human rights through such activities as the release of prisoners of conscience, fair and prompt trials of all political prisoners, and elimination of torture and executions.

The Campaign.   Over a six-week period in October and November 1988, the "Human Rights Now!" world concert tour performed 20 concerts in 16 countries attended by more than one million people. Reebok underwrote expenses through its Reebok Foundation, with a $2-million grant and guarantees against losses of up to $8 million.

To direct marketing and public relations activities for the tour and a continuing program in the human rights arena after its completion, Reebok retained the public relations and marketing firm Cone Communications.

A two-phased PR strategy was formulated. The first consisted of activities in seven international markets to complement and support the tour itself and to reach young people everywhere with its human rights message. The second phase was the creation and launch of an annual Reebok Human Rights Award designed to keep alive the company's commitment to the global cause supported by its primary customers. Activities in both phases were scrupulously governed by using low-key, dignified tactics reflecting sensitivity to the feelings of all who are concerned with human rights.

The Tour.   For the tour Cone assembled and directed a media team that included a radio producer and announcer and a video production team. The two groups staged 17 press conferences worldwide, one in each tour city; prepared and issued on-site audio and video news releases; and shot footage that would later become the tour documentary entitled *Sounds Against Silence.* More than 13,000 journalists and photographers attended the media conferences.

Leading athletes and coaches served as worldwide representatives for Reebok by conducting "chalk talks" on human rights with international sports figures. Radio promotions were aimed at 81 U.S. college campuses. A promotion in teen magazines encouraged use of a Reebok Tour logo. There were spots on 130 teen-oriented radio stations.

Additional activities were designed for retail salespeople and field service representatives, international distributors of Reebok products, and Reebok employees. A quarterly newspaper, *Reebok Backstage,* was produced and distributed to 80,000 of these people. A traveling exhibit on the tour for Reebok employees included a contest for tour concert tickets and backstage passes.

Cooperative ventures arranged with distributors and media outlets resulted in additional worldwide exposure for the tour and its human rights message. The "Human Rights Now!" tour and Reebok's association with it were widely reported by both national and international media.

Internationally, the leading newspapers in each concert city reported Reebok's commitment to human rights. An *International Herald Tribune* feature bore the headline "Reebok's Toe Hold in Rock 'n' Rights."

Over 15 million TV viewers saw coverage of the tour on the ABC *Evening News,* CNN, MTV, HBO, and major network affiliates; audio news reports were carried by 130 teen-oriented radio stations; and 100,000 copies of the *Reebok Backstage* newsletters circulated in 14,000 retail outlets.

The Human Rights Award.   The Reebok Human Rights Award annually confers a $100,000 prize on "outstanding individuals under the age of 30 who have made major contributions to the advancement of human rights." The nine-member international board of advisers that selects the winners includes Reebok International's Chairman Paul Fireman, former U.S. president Jimmy Carter, and other human rights supporters in public life, business, and the arts.

Four winners, two from the United States and two from South Africa, were chosen for the first awards in 1988. And, on December 7, during Human Rights Week, Reebok hosted a formal awards ceremony in New York City, at which Fireman welcomed the guests, and Sen. Edward Kennedy was the keynote speaker. More than 300 human rights supporters attended.

Media interest in the award had been cultivated in advance during contacts with key journalists at the conferences held during the tour. A press kit on the awards ceremony contained biographies of the winners and finalists, a background on the award, and summaries of the human rights situation in various countries. Following the ceremony, a "Frontline Youth Press Conference" brought the award winners together before 200 high school and college journalists.

New human rights opportunities continue to be explored by Reebok. December 1991 commemorated the fifth year of the award.

Corporate Identity through Values.   Cone reports that Reebok-brand awareness around the world has risen as a result of its human rights image (especially among youth—its largest target market). Enhancing its image is the fact that the tour resulted in Amnesty International's worldwide membership increasing by hundreds of thousands.

Reebok's positioning itself as a company with politically "correct" values is mirrored by other companies. Heinz, with its "respect for the family" campaign; Coors, with its championing of literacy; and Toyota, with its advertising series that promotes what it is doing to help its U.S. market advance socially (see Chapter 11), are all embarking on a theme pioneered by Reebok.

"There is a growing number of companies that are talking about establishing a corporate identity through values," observes Linda Lewi, Cone's vice president and group manager. She anticipates that this trend will escalate throughout the 1990s.

Case Example

Apple: Breaking Into the Market

Apple Computer Inc. realized from its very inception that it was not like IBM, it did not want to be like IBM, and it did not want people to think of it like IBM. Rather than trying to imitate the established monolith, Apple redefined for people what they should be looking for in a computer and a computer company. In fact, Apple built its image around the belief that it was better *because* it wasn't IBM.

A pioneer in the personal computer business, Apple entered the market with what it called the "computer for the rest of us." It offered a human-centered machine that brought new meaning to the term "user-friendly." From this concept evolved a corporate culture that came to shape the Apple persona as much as its computers.

The Early Days.   Steve Jobs and his friend Steve Wozniak invented the computer in their garage. It was the American dream of successful individual ingenuity.

The Apple name and logo were created under equally informal circumstances. "I think the idea for the image was to come up with an alternative to the large corporate America image," says Apple's Director of Creative Services Tim Brennan. "Steve Jobs really came up with the name. It was a lot more friendly—'Apple.' That was a revolutionary term for a company, to call it a piece of fruit. It all happened very fast. There wasn't a lot of planning; we didn't pay huge fees to come up with a name for this company. These were all decisions that were made quickly, and luck was involved with a lot of it. For some reason, the name just stuck."

The logo was developed by Regis McKenna, a public relations and marketing consulting firm. "I think the total cost for their logo was something like $500," says Steve Hayden, creative director at BBDO, Apple's current advertising agency. "It was presented to Apple as 'This is all we have at the moment. We're not satisfied with it because it's a six-color logo and it's really quite impractical for a small company. You'll have to run it in color for it to look right and you can't really afford color, but this is the best that we have at the moment.' Steve Jobs got very excited about it and said, 'I don't care—it's great and we want to do great stuff.' "

Internationalization.   Because the company almost immediately began marketing overseas, there was concern about how well the name and logo would translate internationally. But Hayden says that research has proven them to be meaningful in all cultures, with one condition: The name must usually be placed alongside the logo for the connection between the two to be made. "That's because if a Swede or a Frenchman were to simply look at that mark they would come up with a Swedish or French word for Apple, and not the name of the company," he says. "Even in Japan, we signed the ads with the logo and the word Apple."

"The Apple look really evolved in the early 1980s as an alliance between Lee Klow of [the advertising firm] Chiat Day, and Tom Suiter and Tom Hughes, both of Apple Computer," says Hayden. "These three people really began to set the look of Apple packaging systems. They cleaned them up and brought in professional help for the first time. What they wanted to do was to have something like Apple Computers themselves, friendly and inviting, yet precise. I think that's really the core thought of the design systems. Projecting that image internationally has been something of a challenge. But I think the design standards coming out of Cupertino [Apple's headquarters in California] and the packaging manuals, collateral, support materials—even Apple T-shirts—as well as the Apple advertising created by Chiat Day, have been so strong that when we recently pulled together work from Apple in 26 different countries outside the United States, it was remarkably similar in design. It had the same typeface, the same white look to the advertising, the same uncluttered appearance."

Since those early days, the company behind the logo has come to stand for three things: high-quality, easy-to-use products; innovation, including inventive marketing, creative managerial techniques, and an unconventional organizational structure; and employee responsiveness.

"Apple is committed, both in the United States and all around the world, to creating what is often called the third wave—sort of a cutting-edge organizational structure and workplace," explains Christopher Escher, Apple's manager of corporate public relations. "That means a flatter organization, less hierarchy, and a more open, more casual atmosphere. It's usually associated with very high benefits packages and high compensation to employees. These are the three points that are constant and inform everybody's top-level, corporate PR activity, whether they're in Italy or here in California."

An Image Grounded in Reality.   Apple's unique products do much of the talking for the company. As the people who brought computer technology to the common man, Apple was born with a built-in image difference. "The idea was that there's another way to compute; you don't have to be tied to a mainframe," says Brennan. "That's where the whole personal computer revolution started. The business itself really was quite a bit different from the business that IBM was in at the time."

"Apple's technology is very accessible—that was the company's original goal—and I think that its products really are its image out in the marketplace," says Jane Anderson, a principal with Regis McKenna. "People get emotionally involved with the Macintosh, whereas they tend not to get so emotionally attached to an IBM PC."

Word of the company's open style of operation has also gotten around without much conscious effort by Apple. "We used to joke that Apple's got the walk-around style of management because it's very open internally. I think that's reflected on the outside," says Anderson. "Apple has also given the wealth back to the employees—there are a lot of Apple millionaires. I think Apple has the largest stock participation of any company in the *Fortune* 500, and that word spreads, too," she adds.

With the company so much in the public spotlight, the challenge is often to manage its publicity, both the good and the bad, rather than actively seek out more. "Apple is not out to just get its name in the paper," says Anderson. "It's out to educate people and make them understand what the company's about, what it's doing, what the technology's about. I think Apple takes a different approach to communication than most companies."

Developing the Image.   Apple's image has undergone some changes
through the years, mainly because of the company's desire to expand its
appeal to businesses. "In order for the company to grow, we had to find
people who were looking to buy large volumes of computers," says
Brennan. "We had to become a player. You just can't stay 'the computer
for the rest of us' forever. So between 1985 and 1990, the image
changed."

"In other words, that side of the personality had to be added to the
Apple equation," explains Hayden. "That was done by the Macintosh II
family, the introduction of far more powerful Macintosh computers for
business. It was also done by having the advertising project a somewhat
more serious tone that was appealing to business. In the United States, it
involved commercials depicting typical business situations—very serious
business topics. In Sweden, it was turned into a testimonial campaign. In
France, it came out as a philosophy of business campaign."

Although the advertising is still innovative, it has taken on a more
subdued attitude over the years. "It has become much more important
for Apple to fit in, to stand out performance-wise, fit into the corporate
environment and not be the risky investment," Hayden explains. The
tactic seems to have paid off: Almost two-thirds of Macintosh computers
are sold to businesses.

However, the tide may be changing once again. Although Apple does
not plan to abandon the business market it has cultivated, it is reshifting
its focus to its original market. "I think that now we're trying to get back
to the roots," says Brennan. "I think now is the time to say, let's make
those Macintoshes easy to buy and more popular and cheaper. I think
our price points were more targeted at businesses that could afford to
buy $8,000–$10,000 computers. But now we're trying to bring
computers under $1000 to various people's hands again. In order to
do that, we also have to 'un-business' our advertising—take our ties off.
We're going to have to get back into individual situations, a variety of
lifestyles. I think the character of our work is going to change. My
personal opinion is that our work is always going to change. It's like
Halloween—we can be whatever we want to be. That's one of the
advantages of being Apple Computer over being IBM."

The Local Touch.   Besides refining the Apple image, the company
has been working on how it is perceived in different parts of the world.
"Apple is interesting in that it's one part global and one part very local,"
says Bob Spoffert, director of strategic planning for BBDO. "At the
highest level there is a core strategy: who they are, what the basic vision
is, what differentiates the brand from the competition. That is essentially
a global vision. But it translates pretty dramatically into the local
situation from country to country, so it's sort of a 50-50 mix that way."

Apple has relied heavily on its offices around the world to direct
regional advertising, reasoning that they are the ones closest to the local
market and thus are best equipped to determine what's appropriate.

"The development of the personal computer market is unquestionably higher in the United States just in terms of people using them," explains Gene Cameron, CEO of BBDO San Francisco. "There's a recent study that shows that about 30 percent of the people in the United States work on a computer in some fashion daily. In Europe, that number is about 11 percent. That suggests a certain growth path to a market. And so the kind of advertising we're going to be doing in the United States is going to be a little bit more advanced and deal with a different set of issues. In France, for example, our guys decided the U.S. spot was good, but their particular situation needed to have a little bit more of a high-concept piece. So they actually ran two 30-second spots together. First, they ran a French spot that was more about the dreams and aspirations and things you can manage to do with an Apple computer. They followed that with a U.S. execution that talks about how Apple is the computer that people actually use."

The differences in market development correlate with slight variations in Apple's image from country to country. "There are some differences in the maturity of the image," explains Spoffert. "In countries where the share is low or Apple has only recently established itself, they tend to have what was the old U.S. image—very, very heavy on the ease of use, and not terribly well developed in terms of the real capability and potential of the technology. So it tends to be seen as maybe a computer for beginners. In countries where the business and market share has matured and people really understand what the technology is about, then you see something that's closer to what you have in the United States and the more developed markets."

Core Perceptions in a Global Image.   Even so, there are some basic core perceptions about Apple. "I think that Apple is recognized around the world as the human-centered computer," says Hayden. "One of the things that's helped us internationally is the fact that the Macintosh is a purely graphics-based computer, which means that it is very easy to customize to non-English alphabets."

There is also uniformity in the tone of most Apple advertising. "It's a little on the brash side," says Brennan. "There's a certain thing called 'Applease' that we use. It's really a kind of dialogue or copy that is different from other corporations. We try to keep it a little friendlier and livelier—fresher. It goes back to the attitude that we're not big business, even though we're bigger in size now."

Perhaps that is why, even with its efforts to woo the business consumer, the company has always kept its special appeal to youth as well. "The sense of Apple brand being associated with the younger, more innovative generation is pretty consistent around the world," says Spoffert. "It tends to be how Apple gets into the market. The Macintosh is the computer of choice on college campuses, and all those kids graduate from college and bring their Macs with them. They are the agents of change in a lot of businesses."

Finding a Global Voice.   Apple has been taking an increasingly global view of its business lately, including its advertising. "It's an evolutionary thing," says Spoffert. "Apple has had some very large and successful operations outside the United States for quite a while. There are several parts of the world where they literally have a higher market share than they do in the United States and go back almost as far as they do in the United States. But the company is becoming aware that there is a common global direction. With Apple, it'll never be as simple as a Kodak or a Coca-Cola or a Gillette, where you're selling essentially the same thing with the same brand image around the world. But we're getting a bit more of that part of it into the equation. A few years back, our marketing was very, very local. And now the company is becoming somewhat more globally unified."

Because of the international nature of its market as well as the desire for greater communications efficiency, Apple is making a conscious effort to standardize its message around the world. "One thing we're learning through this filter of the local situation is that, again and again, Apple's ability to succeed in the local market comes back to certain things that do seem to be universal. Of course, the idea of empowering the individual in business is going to play up very differently in Japan than it does in the United States or, for that matter, Italy or France. But somehow there's a piece of that core idea behind the acceptance and success of Apple in any one of those places."

One of Apple's primary aims is to try to replace its 26-country advertising setup with a more efficient one. The approach being discussed is to centralize control over corporate advertising while letting product advertising remain localized.

To facilitate this global coordination, both the company and the agency are concentrating on greater communication with their worldwide offices. BBDO meets far more frequently now—usually three times a year—than it did in the past to review Apple's international advertising, discuss common strategies, and decide where to head next. Apple's marketing communications managers have the same kinds of meetings, and usually the agency and the client have representatives at each other's gatherings.

Beyond face-to-face encounters, Apple's and BBDO's U.S. and European headquarters are in constant touch electronically. Both companies have access to each other's global E-mail systems, so they can send documents back and forth quickly. Apple also makes frequent use of teleconferencing.

Globalization does not mean the end to Apple's local flavor, however. Some messages will always have to be tweaked for different cultures. For example, Apple's present tag line, "The power to be your best," has undergone some minor adjustments in various countries. Says Spoffert, "in some languages the idea of individual power just doesn't translate. In fact, in Japan, there's been some advertising where they literally ended up using the word 'power' in English because it just does not translate. In other countries you have to put more of a societal spin on the idea of success or empowerment. The 'power to be your best' is viewed as a little too individualistic, and almost selfish or egotistical. For example, throughout most of Latin America we've tended to use a Spanish slogan that means the power to forge ahead and succeed, but it doesn't necessarily have the individual breaking out of the pack."

Furthermore, even with centralized decisions, Apple wants to continue to get input from across borders. "As you move toward a more global branding and imagery, you still want to have that kind of creative ferment that has bright ideas surfacing from different countries," says Spoffert. "In addition to some things not being appropriate for different markets, you'd lose a tremendous amount of the creative vitality that goes into building the brand now if you didn't. I think the whole world benefits from getting together and seeing a whole roomful of different creative approaches to the same strategy, the same issues."

5
Updating
an Old Image

As companies evolve and adapt new strategies to meet changes in the marketplace, more than a few will think about reworking their existing images. Overhauling an image, however, is not something that lends itself to a quick yes-or-no decision. The idea of making a change can sometimes be spontaneous, occurring when management steps back and, perhaps for the first time, sees what the organization has become, where it is going, where it is strong, and where it is weak. Management may then conclude that the name or image presented to the world for many years no longer serves the best needs of the company in a new global market.

This especially applies to those companies that have so completely altered their business that the original name does not convey to the public who they are or what they do. The corporate name may have remained as the business changed, but the image has become so blurred and confused that the company is on the brink of becoming unrecognizable—a corporate nonentity. This often happens as the result of mergers or acquisitions, as well as new product developments.

Polaroid Corp., for example, is discussing what will happen to its image now that it has introduced a new, electronic laser-driven imaging system for the medical field. (The world associates the Polaroid name and company with the instant-film-developing camera that made it famous.) "How will this system, which we feel will play a major role in hospital imaging in the next decade, be received? What is our brand strategy for the future? What will Polaroid represent in 1999? These questions are currently receiving a great deal of attention in our company," says Sam Yanes, corporate communications director. "We understand that our name is one of our greatest assets. We are confident it can carry a medical breakthrough."

Experts say that even in cases where a new image is justified, it is still difficult to change. For centuries, Sears was one of the great names in U.S. business—well known for being a family department and catalog store. In the late 1970s, when management decided to update the Sears image and business, customers were confused by the move away from "basics" and the mix of retail business with financial services. (Coldwell Banker and Dean Witter Reynolds were acquired. Allstate Insurance was already owned.)

A confused public found it difficult to support Sears in the financial services market, and, according to recent sales figures, also does not seem to be supporting Sears as a retail store. Not having played its century-old heritage to any advantage, Sears seems to be losing its core constituency.

A New Look

On the other hand, some new image campaigns have made the difference between failure and success for a number of companies. Spiegel practically reinvented its catalog business to meet the market of the 1980s by shifting its focus to working women, ages 25–54, with $35,000-plus incomes, a group they reasoned was sure to grow. An unwavering position as an easy way to shop for quality clothing was established: "We're old-fashioned; we make shopping easier."

To ground the image to reality, technology was enlisted to indeed make shopping easy. More than $25 million was spent on merchandise prognostics and control systems. Annual phone orders of $18.7 million were answered, all within 12 seconds. A 99.7% accuracy was reached in next-day order filling. The list goes on. Overall, the strategy, driven by a corporate repositioning, has resulted in a fourfold sales increase between 1980 and 1989.

In the following case studies, the companies profiled examined their contemporary images and decided a change was in order. In the case of Xerox, only time will tell how the rest of the world will accept its play for a new image. Scott Paper, on the other hand, is confident it made the right decision.

Case Example

Xerox: Gambling on "The Document Company"

Some companies spend millions of dollars on campaigns to cement a corporate identity. But Xerox announced in the fall of 1990 that it was going all out to rid itself of one. Len Vickers, Xerox's new senior vice president of worldwide marketing, wants consumers to shift their focus from Xerox's machines to the machines' products—that is, documents and their importance in people's lives. The multilayered communications campaign will position Xerox globally as "The Document Company." Most of the world currently views Xerox (and rather strongly) as a copier company.

As is often the case, the new global image campaign coincides with a new product. On Oct. 2, 1990, Xerox announced the debut of DocuTech Publishing Series, which puts offset-quality printing within reach of the ordinary office desktop. The new product line promises to revamp totally the way thousands of businesses create, print, and distribute documents of all kinds. Office workers can now take information—on a piece of paper, in a computer, or on a desktop—and shape it into new forms to send across the hall or around the world.

A lot is riding on the success of this product. DocuTech is designed to become part of a family of machines that will be Xerox's main revenue producer through the 1990s. Envisioned as three main components, one part, the DocuTech Production Publisher, is priced at $220,000.

New Product, New Image. Xerox, like any company choosing to realign and redefine itself after years of having a solid identity, faces a stiff challenge in changing its image from the familiar to one that is more complex, perhaps even hazy. Image consultants concur that they are not quite certain what "The Document Company" really means. For example, Clive Chajet, chairman and CEO of the image consultant firm Lippincott & Margulies, says, "I suppose a document could be something more than just a copy—but I think it would take a lot of thought to make such a distinction."

Xerox, of course, contends there is a distinction. Making the world aware of the pervasive but hidden significance of the document is the campaign's central challenge.

"First, we want people to rethink the role that documents play in their work and their lives," says Vickers in an interview with Xerox in-house quarterly magazine *Benchmark*. "Second, we want to change the way they think about Xerox. We want them to realize the breadth and scope of our capabilities when it comes to documents."

The company contends that documents represent more than five trillion pages of information a year worldwide—95% of the information with which offices work. Up to half of workers' time is spent on documents, up to 40 percent of many companies' labor costs. Improving office productivity is the prize.

Redefining the Business. When Xerox CEO and President Paul Allaire looks at the 1990s, he sees a common link among the following key business trends:

- A growing emphasis on collaboration among work teams and an attendant rise in interpersonal computing

- A trend away from functionally focused hierarchies and toward a key business process management approach
- An increasing demand, driven by heightened competition and a weakened global economy, to improve white-collar productivity

From Allaire's perspective these trends all center around the document and point to new roles it will play in organizations in the 1990s. He believes that a better understanding of documents to improve quality and office productivity is the number one requirement of business in this decade. If this happens, then the global image of The Document Company will be right on target.

In an interview in *Benchmark,* Allaire says: "As much as 95 percent of all corporate information exists where yesterday's data-processing technology can't reach it—in paper documents. Companies are beginning to ask, 'How am I going to make more effective use of that information? How am I going to create it more efficiently and make it more effective in communicating what it is supposed to? How do I improve the productivity of the people interacting with the information that is in the form of documents?' "

Confirming the Campaign.   Were there any doubts about embarking on what some still consider an elusive image campaign? "I had a strong gut feeling about the idea," says Vickers. Still, he spent several months second-guessing whether The Document Company idea was, in fact, the right idea. "We tested it out on a lot of other people," he adds. "We listened hard to what was in the air." The process assured Vickers and his creative team that this was the right message, and it helped them flesh out the idea as well. Their communications campaign was built around responses and reactions from people inside and outside Xerox and from customers and office workers who were asked to take part in focus groups.

The survey reinforced for Vickers the impact documents have on people's lives at individual, organizational, and global levels. Making people aware of the pervasive but hidden significance of the document is the campaign's central challenge.

"For many people, documents are the product of their labors as well as their most tangible accomplishment," he explains. "For a lot of us, a sense of worth, our personal contribution, and the meaning of our work are wrapped up in documents."

Case Example

Scott Paper: PR Campaign Revives a Stale Image

Public relations should not be overlooked in global image building— even though management often considers it difficult to measure its accomplishments. Indeed, Philadelphia-based Scott Paper Co.'s strategic use of public relations made a significant impact in establishing a strong global image for this more-than-a-century-old U.S. company.

Getting Back in Focus.   Scott is the world's largest manufacturer and marketer of sanitary tissue paper products—primarily bathroom tissue, towels, facial tissues, and napkins—with over $5 billion in sales in more than 60 countries, plants in 21 countries, and about 31,000 employees. It also is a leading producer of coated and uncoated printing and publishing paper.

Although aspects of the public relations function have existed at Scott for most of its history, public relations in its current form has been practiced only since 1980. At that time, the company developed a broad-based state and federal government relations function in the United States, a political action committee (PAC), an investor relations program, a model program of corporate social investment, an international public affairs consulting activity, and an award-winning employee communications program.

"The program was started because Scott was in trouble," explains Philip Webster, then vice president of public affairs. (Today he is president of his own firm, The Webster Group, a Wayne, Pennsylvania public affairs and corporate communications consulting firm.) "In the mid-1960s, Scott had lost its leadership position in the industry, lost market share, and become unfocused," says Webster. "Its costs were too high, and its profits too low. Its stock price reflected this, as did employee morale."

Leadership Supportive of PR Campaign.   Management elected a new CEO, who was willing to become a partner in the public relations process. His goal was to change the company's fortune and its culture. He worked with the staff in developing a strategic communications and advocacy program directed to all of Scott's publics.

Webster continues, "Although the ideal would have been to develop a master strategic plan for all public relations and then implement it, Scott's program actually developed function by function, in response to emerging crises and priorities. It began with the establishment of an investor relations program after a Canadian company acquired 25 percent of Scott and wanted more, and after management recognized its common stock was significantly undervalued. Several harmful strikes provided the impetus to develop an employee communications program in which more than 30 publications at the corporate, operating group, and local plant level communicated common strategic themes regularly to employees at all levels."

Government support was deemed critical to achieving the company's strategic plan. To this end, state and federal government relations programs were put into motion, such as the building of a PAC and the opening of a Washington, D.C. office. The international public affairs consulting practice grew as well when several of Scott's international companies needed help to solve critical strategic problems and turned to the Public Affairs Division to find solutions.

Even in the absence of a master plan for public relations, the company emerged with an effective, well-coordinated program because of its results-oriented approach.

"From the beginning, once Scott decided to take the public relations initiative in a particular area, it did so strategically, supported by research, planning, and involvement by many players within the company who would be critical to the program's success. Although each public relations program was born of a reaction to an external event or events, the company did conclude that public relations must be proactive on an ongoing basis, rather than reactive. Scott decided that managing change, rather than being managed by it, would give it a greater degree of control over its destiny," explains Webster.

Analyzing the Bottom-Line Impact. A proponent of holding public relations accountable for meaningful results, Webster encouraged senior executives to look at the program with an eye to the bottom line.

How was this done? First, in government relations, Scott identified and acted principally on issues that would affect its profits and losses margins. It kept track of dollar impact on a quarterly and yearly basis and found that proactive advocacy efforts saved the company tens of millions of dollars annually. The government-relations program helped defeat legislation that would have had a negative impact on cash flow, and it helped pass bills into law that augmented the company's cash flow.

"One provision in a federal tax bill, for example, allowed Scott to sell its unused investment tax credits for approximately $135 million. Another law initiated by Scott, the Pennsylvania Shareholder Protection Act, raised the barrier level for corporate raiders," says Webster. "Two others, the Alabama and Pennsylvania Cogeneration Acts, allowed the company to build facilities to generate its own electrical power while receiving favorable compensation rates for the excess power it created."

In the investor-relations area, a broad-based communications program reaching out to the worldwide investment community produced extraordinary results. "Because of strong quarter-by-quarter earnings, the company's stock increased almost sixfold over six years and outperformed the Standard & Poor's 500 by over 150 percent," says Webster.

He continues: "Shareholders received more than $2.6 billion in enhanced value from the increased stock price, as well as a significantly higher dividend payout. And, most important, the Canadian company that owned 25 percent of Scott agreed to sell its stock back to the company, its takeover bid stymied—partially because of the dramatically increased stock price, partially because of the previously mentioned new Shareholder Protection Act."

In the third area, employee communications, Scott recognized that its strategies in the 1960s and 1970s had lacked focus, and launched an effort to determine the company's mission or vision for the future. That mission was then communicated through a pyramid system of more than 30 interrelated publications to employees, from the corporate offices to the plant floor.

"Common strategic themes—such as reducing cost and improving productivity, quality, and customer satisfaction—were articulated over and over again by the CEO to his employees," says Webster. "The result, over time, was a dramatic increase in operating margins. Employees' morale and pride in their company grew, supported by a program that made every domestic employee a shareholder of the company."

Guidelines to Updating an Old Image

Scott's program demonstrates several of the important points that are crucial in keeping a company out of the image doldrums. According to Webster:

- *The program must be planned, rather than "ad hoc."* Scott's initiatives in each area were built on carefully constructed strategic plans designed to achieve specific image-enhancing goals.

- *The program must be aligned with overall corporate goals.* Scott's public relations activity helped to create shareholder value, improve sales and profits, build market share, enhance the company's reputation, improve productivity, and build employee alignment—all corporate goals.

- *Whenever possible, the program should be proactive.* Scott took the initiative, in many cases plowing new ground, in carrying out its public relations activities.

- *Results should be quantifiable.* They will often exceed the resources being invested in the public relations program. Scott saved or made tens of millions of dollars annually because of the program and what it accomplished.

- *Many people outside of public relations should contribute to the program's success.* All should be made to feel like partners in the effort, sharing both in the creation of the program and in the credit it receives.

- *PR must have the support of the CEO and senior management.* Without that, any endeavors are almost guaranteed to fail.

Crisis Management and Social Causes

- *Crisis management.* The revamped image campaign also led to an examination of the company's crisis management program. Many corporations have learned that public relations activity can prepare and provide value to the company in times of emergency.

    "Top management asked public relations to develop and implement a strategy to persuade a union local to discontinue a nine-month strike that had cost Scott about $9 million. Within three weeks of coalescing public opinion against the workers, the strike ended," says Webster. "Employees returned to work with a contract substantially the same as that offered nine months earlier."

    In Mexico, a Scott affiliate was caught in an economic "Catch-22," with the peso being devalued and inflation running at extremely high rates. Price controls went into effect. The company was losing millions of dollars and was unable to raise prices to offset rising costs. "Public relations moved in to counsel Mexican management on how to motivate government authorities to loosen their price controls on the company and its industry," says Webster. "In a matter of weeks, the government allowed appropriate price increases, and profit margins returned to normal."

- *Social responsibility.* In another area—social responsibility—Scott shifted its program's focus from philanthropy to targeted social investment, expecting the program to earn a return for both the company and its communities. The result: A range of company resources—funds, knowledge, and experience, and employee and retiree volunteerism—was used to make a difference in the communities where the corporation is located.

    "Aspects of the model program were recognized twice by then President Ronald Reagan with presidential citations for private sector initiatives. And the company's reputation was enhanced in its plant communities because it leveraged its support for critical social issues from which others shied away," explains Webster.

    Updating its stale image in the social-responsibility area led Scott to broaden its activities into cause-related marketing. Public Affairs, for example, assisted in the creation and commercialization of Helping Hand, a product line designed both to assist charity and to gain profitable volume and market share for the company. "In its first 18 months," notes Webster, "the promotion increased shelf space, market share, and volume for Scott; it also contributed more than $1.6 million to six charities that helped children with special needs."

    The effort evolved into an annual event, through which purchases of Scott products benefit Ronald McDonald Houses, which support families of critically ill children during their hospital stays. "The promotion was the most successful in the company's history, generating significantly increased volume and profit, providing favorable nationwide recognition for Scott and raising nearly $8 million to date for the Ronald McDonald Houses in the United

States," says Webster. He adds, "Along the way, it also helped Scott build a business relationship with McDonald's—which, with 18 million customers daily, goes through huge amounts of paper napkins, bathroom tissue, and tray liners."

■ *Consumer relations.* One last example of what image building can do for a company lies in the consumer-relations area. Scott recognized that an enduring and growing consumer franchise was a critical ingredient for competitive advantage. "It looked to public relations to create systems to encourage consumer interaction with the company. The main thrust of the program was a toll-free number promoted on all of the company's packaging to encourage consumers to express both positive and negative views to the company," explains Webster.

"The goal was to build consumer support. Today, Scott's consumer franchise is stronger than ever. In addition, the information gathered has been invaluable to brand managers, and the interchange with consumers has allowed the company to cross-market its products," he says.

6

Tinkering with the Tried and True

A few products are so well known and have such strongly defined images that tampering with them is bound to be dangerous. While there are many examples of failed campaigns to change the image of well-established products, none is as notorious as the "New Coke" failure.

In 1985, the reformulated Coke failed, despite huge promotional spending, because Coca-Cola tinkered with one of the best-loved images in the world—that of original Coke. (That image is number one in terms of recognition in the United States and Europe and number 17 in Japan, according to Landor Associates' ImagePower Survey.) Consumers simply did not want to replace the original, and Coke executives had ignored research that stated this. Coke was forced to spend many millions of dollars reintroducing its original formulation and "buying back" consumers' nostalgia. Classic Coke is the name of a classic image—and it has become the symbol of a classic marketing error.

As the Coke story suggests, companies should research what the market wants—and heed that research. This means not being afraid to stick with the original product, if that is what the consumer prefers.

Nevertheless, there *are* instances when images must be changed regardless of the consequences. This is true for the two companies described next. Both make and sell products with strong worldwide images: Waterford crystal and Jaguar automobiles. Both have to alter their tried-and-true product lines not because they think a new image is needed, but because of tough financial circumstances.

77

Case Example

Waterford Wedgwood: Gambling on Lower-Priced Crystal

In 1986, Waterford Crystal of Ireland bought Wedgwood, the venerable British chinamaker. (Today the company is known as Waterford Wedgwood PLC.) Ever since, the china division has propped up the unprofitable crystal division. Accounting errors, management turnover, high union wages, and a strong Irish pound have all contributed to the crystal division's continuing losses. In light of these problems and to get back into the black, management decided it could no longer afford to sell only the classically designed, handcrafted, expensive crystal for which it is known around the globe.

Targeting New Consumers.   It's lonely at the top of the line. That's what Waterford Wedgwood determined about its place in the crystal market. In late 1990, the company began test marketing a new, lower-priced line in the United States. The move, intended to appeal to more contemporary tastes and thinner wallets, was prompted by the firm's desire to expand its share of the premium crystal market in the United States.

"Waterford competes in about 30 percent of the market, but we have no products to offer at all in the other 70 percent," explains Redmond O'Donoghue, sales and marketing director for Waterford. "That leaves us the option to either say goodbye to that business or to attack it. Our choice is the latter."

The target market segment consists mainly of younger consumers, including brides, who appreciate the Waterford brand name but find its traditional glassware designs too conservative. "Their preference is for something lighter and more contemporary, or at least more transitional, in design terms," notes O'Donoghue. "We feel we have an obligation, both to ourselves as businesspeople and to our consumers, to offer them what they want."

In April 1991, Waterford introduced the Marquis by Waterford Crystal line to fill that obligation. Marquis stemware was scheduled to be in stores by August 1991, priced from $29 to $37.50 per stem, compared with the regular Waterford line, which started at $49.50. O'Donoghue describes the price range of the new line as "moderate, but not cheap. Waterford would never be associated with the lower end. In fact, these are price points we used to sell at five or six years ago, but had to vacate because our cost structure was up."

Although the crystal maker abandoned the machine manufacturing techniques that it had originally been interested in using for the new line, it did leave its traditional production base in Waterford, Ireland, finding cheaper labor for the new line in Yugoslavia, Germany, and Portugal. Each piece of Marquis crystal will be marked with its country of origin.

Shattering an Image?   The risk of Marquis to Waterford's image is twofold: the damage that could be done by introducing a lower-priced product, and the abandonment of its namesake town for producing the new line. Since the company's founding, every piece of crystal has been made by hand in the town of Waterford. Moreover, the company has proudly trumpeted this heritage in its advertising, citing it as an integral aspect of Waterford's superior quality.

O'Donoghue insists that the new line will not tarnish the established Waterford image: "We recognize that one of the most precious things we have at Waterford is our brand name, and we would do nothing to endanger it. All our actions are supported by market research that we carried out intensively throughout 1990 to ensure that we wouldn't take a wrong step."

He adds that the traditional Waterford line will be kept intact, with no changes in price or production location: "We see this as an incremental business situation. The creation of the new line does not mean for a minute that the traditional, classic Waterford glass won't continue to come from Waterford, Ireland. It will. We are dedicated to building that business as well. But we also want to attack those price points where we are not competing at the moment." He points out that the company is exercising great care to prevent the new items from cannibalizing Waterford's existing market.

A Competitor's Philosophy.   Whatever the merits of Waterford's new approach, the company's biggest competitor, Baccarat, is not rushing to follow suit. Patrick Baboin, sales director for France's Cie. des Cristalleries Baccarat, says, "We would not consider coming out with a more moderate line, because the only way we could price the product more moderately would be to compromise on quality. Baccarat crystal could not be manufactured outside the town of Baccarat, because we would never get the same quality elsewhere. Our workers have centuries of experience, and they know the Baccarat philosophy of perfect quality."

Baboin feels that the origin of the product is tied not only to its quality, but also to the *image* of that quality in the public's mind. By this reasoning, even if the same standards were used to produce the crystal elsewhere, consumers would believe the product to be inferior.

Distinct Lines.   Clive Chajet of Lippincott & Margulies is more optimistic about Waterford's plan. "My guess is that the least part of Waterford's image is based on the fact that it's made in Ireland. That's a guess, but since Ireland per se doesn't bring any particular cachet to glassmaking techniques, I don't think it's terribly important. I would be much more concerned about the lower price." Nevertheless, Chajet believes that if the situation is handled correctly, both the premium and the moderately priced lines can coexist.

Creating a different name for the new line was a smart decision, he says, and will be helpful in preserving the Waterford image. However, he disagrees with Waterford's decision to sell the two lines through the same outlets: "Separate channels of distribution could certainly help reduce any possible damage to the traditional Waterford line."

Chajet concurs with the company's plans to present the new line as an addition to, not a substitute for, its traditional crystal. "I think it has to be positioned as providing the consumer with a choice of Waterfords. Not that one is necessarily better than the other, but that there's a choice, just as with so many other fine brand names.

"This is obviously an attempt by Waterford to leverage its brand image and the awareness of the brand name, which is, I would assume, very high within the target market. I'm almost tempted to say, this is so natural, why didn't they do it before? All powerful brands—and Waterford is a powerful brand—have line extensions to expand their base. And if it doesn't make sense to do it from Ireland, well, that's a manufacturing issue."

Larry Ackerman, a partner with the identity consulting firm, Anspach Grossman Portugal, injects a note of caution. He believes that any time a company tinkers with an established image it is taking a risk. "How Waterford management positions the second line will make the difference. Establishing the line as a separate brand will help alleviate any blurring between the products. Using a new name will help in this regard. All this will have an effect on the market response."

The Union View.   As might be expected when jobs are at stake, Waterford's labor unions have taken a very strong stand against the new manufacturing and marketing strategy. There are rumors that the unions intend to launch a disparaging publicity campaign in the United States, warning people to beware of the lower-quality goods. To date, these rumors have not been substantiated.

O'Donoghue acknowledges the unions' fear that the new line threatens Waterford's established business and, thus, their jobs. "Hopefully, with some time, we can prove to them that this is not substitution, it's incrementalism," he says.

Waterford's union leader Walter Cullen says he already understands this and still disagrees with management's vision. "They are taking a huge gamble with the Waterford image. Our loyal customers—especially in the United States—are willing to pay high prices for our products because they are hand-blown here in Waterford."

Cullen says that the union is working with management to produce a separate line of Waterford that can be hand-blown in Ireland to meet the price range demanded by a less-affluent market. "This way, the company will be able to offer a line that is a little less expensive, but will not have to be labeled 'made in Portugal,' or wherever. The Waterford image will not be destroyed." To date, no decision has been reached on the union's proposals.

Chajet says the company must come up with a suitable response to the union's complaints. "It should have an appropriate advertising campaign or some sort of communications program saying up front that this is not Irish made, but that it has nothing to do with any diminution of Ireland's ability to design and manufacture beautiful glassware."

That seems to be what Waterford has been planning all along. Although the company has not finalized details of its advertising campaign, its April announcement made no apologies for the new production locations. Says O'Donoghue, "We're going to take the high road with this. We're not going to have any secrets. There'll be no absence of credibility, nothing furtive about it. It will be an up-front product offering, which we believe certain consumers will welcome."

Case Example

Jaguar: Going for Higher Volume

The Jaguar automobile has long symbolized speed, power, and beauty. Practically handmade in the United Kingdom, the car has a mystique all its own, one that is capable of inducing customers to part with upwards of $60,000 for the XJ-S convertible—even though the public's perception of the car is not one of unquestioned quality or consistent performance.

Despite its outstanding image, unfavorable currency movements had been eating away at the company's profits, leaving it vulnerable to takeover. Finally, the Ford Motor Co. acquired the financially ailing luxury auto manufacturer in November 1989 for $2.5 billion. Ford had long been looking for a car that it could use to position itself as a high-end European car manufacturer. The lofty price represents a very large bet by Ford on the value of Jaguar's well-defined global image and Ford's ability to use this to market advantage. Indeed, many analysts say the price Ford paid was at least $1 billion too much (at the time of purchase, Jaguar PLC had about $1.6 billion in revenues).

Ford's Rationale.   As a global company, Ford sells more and derives a larger share of its profits in Europe than in the United States. In 1989, Ford Britain reported after-tax profits of $699 million on sales of $9.4 billion. The only high-end car it had, prior to its purchase of Jaguar, was the Lincoln, which never did well in Europe.

Ford had been exploring opportunities to boost its presence in the luxury auto market for some time. The urgency of doing so increased after the entry of the Japanese into the fray with cars such as Infiniti and Lexus. Ford's acquisition of Jaguar represented an important step toward fulfilling this goal—and, by some observers' reckoning, enabled

Ford to practically leapfrog over the Japanese, who had to start from scratch to build a luxury image for its offerings.

"Everybody talks about whether we paid too much for Jaguar. But look at what we got—a prestigious name and entry in a segment we were not in," said Ford Motor Chairman Harold Poling in an interview with *Automotive News* following the acquisition. "And you ask yourself, 'What would it take to duplicate that from ground zero?' We bought one of the most prestigious names in the world—all over the world—not just in North America or Europe, but in Japan, Australia, Taiwan."

"The Jaguar name certainly gets attention," says one Wall Street auto analyst. "It's also a way for owners to distinguish themselves from the many owners of Mercedes and BMWs on the road, especially in the crowded European market."

Ford and Jaguar both believe that there is considerable potential to increase sales volume by expanding Jaguar's product line in Europe, the United States, and other parts of the world. To do this, Jaguar will need greater resources than it currently has—but which Ford intends to supply. These include substantial financing, which will enable Jaguar to accelerate new product development and provide access to a worldwide technology and components base. Some auto market watchers say that the combination of Ford's tough-minded management and Jaguar's image may turn out to be one of the cleverer business deals of the decade.

Maintaining the Image.   Ford executives are very concerned that the Jaguar image not suffer because the cars are now part of the Ford group. Ford is taking several steps to ensure that this does not happen.

First, Jaguar will remain a separate legal entity, with a self-sustaining capital structure and its own board of directors. The board, which will operate independently within agreed financial-control parameters, will comprise senior Jaguar managers, Ford-nominated directors, and independent nonexecutive directors.

Second, Jaguar will report organizationally to the chairman of Ford Europe. Third, Jaguar's corporate headquarters will remain in Coventry. Fourth, manufacturing facilities in the West Midlands will be modernized and expanded.

Finally, Jaguar's existing management team and employees—the skilled craftspeople who painstakingly build Jaguars piece by piece—will continue to be fully responsible for the day-to-day operation of the company.

But sensitivity to the need for image preservation may not be enough. Some skeptics say the change of ownership heralds the end of Jaguar. "Ford's enormous costs to acquire Jaguar must by necessity mean it will have to start mass-producing the cars in order to make a profit," says John Casesa, an auto-industry analyst at Wertheim Schroder & Co. "When the volume of Jaguar's production triples to make money back for Ford, the brand will suffer. It won't be the Jaguar that people are willing to spend so much for now."

Ford may indeed be planning for substantially greater production volume. The groundwork is being laid for a manufacturing expansion that could almost quadruple Jaguar's output by the end of the decade—to almost 200,000 cars a year from approximately 50,000 made in 1990. With such a large number of Jaguars in the offing, the car's cachet may well be damaged. The image of the sleek, sporty roadster practically made by hand for 67 years in the creaking factories of Coventry could quickly give way to an image of just another high-priced but mass-produced automobile.

Image consultant Clive Chajet thinks the change in ownership must be handled very carefully from an image perspective. "If Jaguar winds up being perceived as an expensive Ford, the magic of the brand will be seriously diminished. How the brand will be distributed—through a Ford dealer network or a more select group—will have a major impact on Jaguar's image."

7

Adjusting to New
Global Pressures

The emergence of such important world problems as global warming and ozone depletion creates a new type of image challenge for companies. Previously, environmental issues were linked to specific, highly sensitive industries, such as chemicals and oil. Now every sector must take stock of its relationship to the environment.

Global companies should prepare for environmental challenges from two fronts: government regulatory policy and public activism. As EC Commissioner for the Environment, Carlo Ripa di Meana declared: "Industrialists are coming to recognize that they can no longer fall back on the well-worn arguments of profitability and efficiency being incompatible with environmental protection. These arguments are irrelevant in a world where the consumer is increasingly ready to pay for environmentally friendly products."

Food packaging, autos, detergents, and paper are some of the consumer products that have been most affected. But all companies are expected to feel the impact of the growing environmental movement. Those that are able to project an awareness of their obligation to defend the environment will boost their global image. The companies detailed here—McDonald's Corp., Dow Chemical, and Johnson & Johnson—address how they are building a friend-to-the-environment image.

Case Example

McDonald's Corp.: Turning the Tide
on the Throwaway Mentality

When the world thinks of McDonald's, it thinks of fast food. Unfortunately, this image carries with it the onus of seeming to be a perpetuator of the "throwaway" mentality—a difficult image to live with in a conservation-conscious age. Recognizing how important it was to the company that it shed this identity, in April 1991 McDonald's announced its comprehensive Waste Reduction Action Plan.

The Plan contains 42 discrete initiatives, pilot projects, and tests for reducing solid waste in the areas of source reduction, reuse, recycling, and composting that McDonald's will undertake within the next two years. Included is the repackaging of its hamburger products from the plastic foam "clamshell" boxes to paper packaging. In addition, McDonald's outlined its "Commitment to the Environment" (see pp. 88–89). Although initially instituted in the United States, the plan is expected to affect all 12,000 McDonald's restaurants in 55 countries.

Alliance with the EDF.   The decision to embark on its waste reduction campaign came largely as a result of an unusual alliance forged last August between the company and the Environmental Defense Fund (EDF). Headquartered in New York, the EDF is a national nonprofit organization that links science, economics, and law to create innovative, economically viable solutions to environmental problems. It had been known for using aggressive legal tactics to pursue its environmental goals. This time, instead of taking McDonald's to court, the EDF decided to work with the company to further reduce waste and establish a clearer understanding of environmental considerations. Frederic Krupp, the EDF's executive director, contacted Ed Rensi, CEO of McDonald's USA, to discover how the EDF and McDonald's could explore ways in which the company could become less wasteful and more environmentally sensitive.

At the outset, the EDF recognized McDonald's substantial existing initiatives in recycling, and McDonald's interests in going further. McDonald's acknowledged the EDF's expertise in solid waste management and the importance of seeking expert opinions. In undertaking the project, the company committed itself to an unprecedented level of scrutiny by an outside organization.

In August 1990, McDonald's and EDF forged a seven-member task force, made up of several experts from each organization. Most of the task force's work was done in the following six months. The task force was considered to be the first of its kind involving a leading environmental organization and the largest food service corporation in the world. In order to maintain the independence of both parties, the agreement that established the task force included several protections, including a provision that each side pay its own expenses.

"The results of the task force far exceeded all of our expectations and original goals," says Keith Magnuson, McDonald's director of operations development and a task force member. "We started out to study waste reduction options. Instead, we developed a comprehensive waste reduction plan that is already being implemented. The willingness of both McDonald's and the EDF to set aside stereotypes and put expertise and experience to work on finding solutions led to such an aggressive plan."

As further explained by Terri Capatosto, McDonald's director of communications and also a member of the task force, "The decisions the company made were based on environmental benefit—and not their public relations value. In order to be an environmental company, you must make decisions on the basis of good science, not popular trends."

The Task Force Work Process.   The task force realized that it would need a common basis for evaluating and comparing the waste reduction options that could be adopted by McDonald's. Members, therefore, agreed to the following five criteria to evaluate any solid waste management options: (1) consistency with the waste management hierarchy of reduce, reuse, recycle (compost), incinerate/landfill; (2) the magnitude of environmental impact resulting from a change; (3) public health and safety effects; (4) practicality; and (5) economic costs and benefits, both to McDonald's and to the public. These criteria were used with the understanding that the nature of McDonald's business is to serve hot, fresh food in high volumes quickly and efficiently to in-store and take-out customers.

To develop a waste reduction plan, the task force examined in detail the way materials were used and how solid waste was handled in McDonald's U.S. operations, including its restaurants, distribution centers, and suppliers. It took broader environmental impacts into consideration, in part to ensure that changes resulting in solid waste reductions would not create or exacerbate other negative environmental impacts.

Numerous hours were spent in various McDonald's restaurants, and the EDF task force members each worked in a restaurant for a day. The task force benefited from the willingness of McDonald's and its suppliers to open their doors for a review of their operations. Members toured the facilities of two McDonald's food suppliers, five packaging suppliers, and one of the company's largest distribution centers. The task force also visited Plastics Again, a polystyrene recycling facility in Massachusetts, and Resource Conservation Services, a composting facility in Maine. Most of these visits included tours, formal presentations, and extensive question-and-answer sessions with top management and technical experts.

During the course of the project, McDonald's brought in experts from various departments to discuss issues with the task force. Likewise, additional EDF staff provided expertise on issues beyond solid waste, as did experts from other environmental organizations.

McDonald's Corporation: Our Commitment to the Environment

McDonald's believes it has a special responsibility to protect our environment for future generations. This responsibility is derived from our unique relationship with millions of consumers worldwide—whose quality of life tomorrow will be affected by our stewardship of the environment today. We share their belief that the right to exist in an environment of clean air, clean earth, and clean water is fundamental and unwavering.

We realize that in today's world a business leader must be an environmental leader as well. Hence our determination to analyze every aspect of our business for its impact on the environment, and to take actions beyond what is expected if they hold the prospect of leaving future generations an environmentally sound world. We will lead, both in word and in deed.

Our environmental commitment and behavior is guided by the following principles:

Effectively Managing Solid Waste. We are committed to taking a "total lifecycle" approach to solid waste, examining ways of reducing materials used in production and packaging, as well as diverting as much waste as possible from the solid waste stream. In doing so, we will follow three courses of action: reduce, reuse, and recycle.

- *Reduce.* We will take steps to reduce the weight and/or volume of packaging we use. This may mean eliminating packaging, adopting thinner and lighter packaging, changing manufacturing and distribution systems, adopting new technologies, or using alternative materials. We will continually search for materials that are environmentally preferable.

- *Reuse.* We will implement reusable materials whenever feasible within our operations and distribution systems as long as they do not compromise our safety and sanitation standards, customer service and expectations, or are offset by other environmental or safety concerns.

- *Recycle.* We are committed to the maximum use of recycled materials in the construction, equipping, and operations of our restaurants. We are already the largest user of recycled paper in our industry, applying it to such items as tray liners, happy meal boxes, carry-out bags and trays, and napkins.

Through our "McRecycle" program, we maintain the industry's largest store of information on recycling suppliers, and will spend a minimum of $100 million a year on the use of recycled materials of all kinds. We are also committed to recycling and/or composting as much of our solid waste as possible. We will change the composition of our packaging, where feasible, to enhance recyclability.

Conserving and Protecting Natural Resources. We will continue to take aggressive measures to minimize energy and other resource consumption through increased efficiency and conservation. We will not permit the destruction of rain forests for our beef supply. This policy is strictly enforced and closely monitored.

Encouraging Environmental Values and Practices. Given our close relationship with local communities around the world, we believe we have an obligation to promote sound environmental practices by providing educational materials in our restaurants and working with teachers in the schools.

We intend to continue to work in partnership with our suppliers in the pursuit of these policies. Our suppliers will be held accountable for achieving mutually established waste reduction goals, as well as continuously pursuing sound production practices that minimize environmental impact. Compliance with these policies will receive consideration in evaluating suppliers.

Ensuring Accountability Procedures. We understand that a commitment to a strong environmental policy begins with leadership at the top of an organization. Therefore, our environmental affairs officer will be given broad-based responsibility to ensure adherence to these environmental principles throughout our system. This officer will report to the board of directors on a regular basis regarding progress made toward specific environmental initiatives.

Of all the above, we are committed to timely, honest, and forthright communications with our customers, shareholders, suppliers, and employees. And we will continue to seek the counsel of experts in the environmental field. By maintaining a productive, ongoing dialogue with all of these stakeholders, we will learn from them and move ever closer to doing all we can to preserve and protect the environment.

Highlights of McDonald's Action Plan.   The following points
represent 19 out of 42 solid waste reduction initiatives in McDonald's
Waste Reduction Action Plan:

Immediate Initiatives

- Complete the phase-in of brown, 100 percent recycled carry-out bags
  with a minimum of 50 percent post-consumer content by April 1991.
  Big Mac wrap is now made with unbleached paper.
- Complete the implementation of corrugated paper recycling in
  McDonald's U.S. restaurants nationwide by the end of 1991.
- Ensure that all suppliers meet McDonald's 1989 directive to reduce
  overall solid waste by 15 percent by December 1991.
- Ensure that all McDonald's suppliers are using corrugated boxes that
  contain at least 35 percent recycled content by December 1991.
- Incorporate the waste reduction packaging specifications into all
  packaging decisions, with weight equal to other established criteria.
  These specifications will be communicated to all suppliers by June 1991.
- Eliminate cutlery packaging where local health codes allow.

Ongoing Commitments

- Use unbleached paper products, or products that are made with more
  benign bleaching paper processes, wherever feasible.
- Annually evaluate all shipping packaging to determine items that
  could be eliminated or reduced.
- Make changes as needed in packaging composition in all materials
  used to enhance recycling or composting initiatives.
- Continue to purchase a minimum of $100 million of recycled
  materials of all kinds each year for use in restaurant operations and
  construction through McRecycle USA.

Ongoing and Near-term Tests

- Conduct a pilot test for recycling post-consumer, paper-based food
  packaging in spring 1991.
- Conduct a series of composting tests to assess the feasibility of
  composting organic and paper waste starting in March 1991.
- Conduct a test of a starch-based material for consumer cutlery to
  replace present plastic cutlery to evaluate its functionality and
  compostability.
- Test refillable coffee mugs and pump-style bulk condiment dispensers
  in place of individual packets by December 1991.
- Test reusable salad lids in restaurants and reusable shipping pallets in
  a distribution center during 1991.

Long-term Research and Development

- Replace disposable corrugated boxes with reusable shipping
  containers wherever possible.
- Seek alternatives to the present wax coatings used on meat shipping
  boxes to enhance their recyclability.

- Explore more recyclable or compostable alternatives for the polyethylene component of the present layered paper sandwich wrap.
- Maximize the use of post-consumer recycled content in all packaging wherever possible, available, and allowable under existing regulations.

Addressing Customer Sensibilities.   CEO Ed Rensi says that the company is adjusting to meet the demands of a more environmentally sensitive public. "Although some scientific studies indicate that foam packaging is environmentally sound, our customers just don't feel good about it. So we're changing."

The EDF was only one of many public voices trying to get McDonald's to change its ways. A few U.S. cities (Portland, Oregon; Berkeley, California; and Newark, New Jersey) have banned containers that are not biodegradable or cannot be recycled. Countless smaller towns are considering similar legislation.

Not everyone is happy about McDonald's policy banishing polystyrene from its food packaging. Companies producing the material—including Mobil Corp., Jen-Pak, and Huntsman Chemical—stand to lose because of the decision. Jerry Johnson, executive director of the Polystyrene Packaging Council, reports that this "came as a shock to us." Others have accused McDonald's of caving in to the environmentalist pressures. Be that as it may, the company feels it made the right choice and intends to stand by it.

"Our decision to switch to this thinner wrap was based on more than three years of research and development of alternative materials," says Capatosto. "This was before the McDonald's–EDF alliance. In addition, the significant benefit of this new paper wrap (over both polystyrene and paperboard, which had been the only available materials) helped us address environmental issues as well as our customers' concerns. We found a way to do what's right for the environment and our customers, and that's simply good for business."

Case Example

Dow Chemical Co.: Overcoming a Bad Image

From an image standpoint, being a chemical company is enough of a disadvantage, but if your firm has manufactured Agent Orange and Napalm (chemicals used in the Vietnam War) and has released cancer-related dioxin, you've got a real challenge on your hands.

By the early 1980s, Dow Chemical Co. had hit rock bottom in the public relations arena: The media, the government, and many consumer and environmental watchdog groups had become the enemy. Aware of the problem, in 1983 Dow gave the situation a good, hard look, took a deep breath, and adjusted its attitude dramatically to remove the sizable chip from its corporate shoulder.

The company's approach to dealing with the public took a 180-degree turn: Management now stresses open communications and a willingness to listen. A full-blown public relations plan and a $65 million advertising campaign were launched to let people know about the positive things Dow does. Finally, Dow employees of all kinds were involved in the communications effort.

The Need to Change.   Dow's actions were a response not only to years of conflict with outsiders over its environmental and ethical record, but also to a shift in its strategic direction. Dow had historically been known as a "chemical company's chemical company." It made staple commodity products, such as chlorine and ethylene, which were sold to other chemical companies around the world. But, by about 1980, management decided to pursue a more balanced product mix, including consumer goods and recession-resistant pharmaceuticals. The new association with products such as Ziploc bags and Fantastik spray cleaner, as well as prescription drugs, required that the company become more palatable to the general public.

Gradually, Dow came to see that it would not win the hearts and minds of U.S. consumers with scientific facts alone. "Dow realizes now that it can't just stand on its science and say, 'Well, we've studied this thing to death, believe us, we're right and we have the data,' " says Cindy Newman, manager of environmental and science communication at Dow. "That's not the way to win trust or credibility."

Jerry Olszewski, managing director at Ketchum Public Relations, Dow's PR agency, recalls the incident that finally pushed the company into action: a 1983 congressional subcommittee hearing in Washington, D.C., on dioxin releases in Midland, Michigan, Dow's hometown.

"Dow went to that hearing armed with very good scientific information and came to the realization that those facts were not really what people were complaining about. They were very much disturbed because they felt the industry simply did not listen to public concerns. In the course of that hearing, Dow was really raked over the coals and held out as a symbol of the antagonism that the public has for the chemical industry," says Olszewski.

He continues, "It was a very eye-opening experience for the company. It was evident to Dow that it was not enough to have good facts, good science; you also had to listen to people, bring them into the process, help them understand what it is you do, and address some of that mistrust that's out there. I think most of the people at Dow would point to that as the experience where they concluded as a company that that was enough. They didn't want to continue being in an adversarial position with all these audiences, ranging from the media to regulators and legislators."

Task Force Reports Dismal Image.   Management's response was to appoint a 12-member task force to survey and study Dow's image among its employees, customers, the media, federal and state government, and the scientific community.

The conclusion was dismal: Dow was seen as a callous and cavalier company that had no interest in cooperating with concerned outside parties. Moreover, the tendency for Dow personnel to take criticism of their company personally was exacting a toll on employee morale.

"The real truth of the matter," explains Olszewski, "is that Dow people had a long history of behavior on most environmental issues that was highly responsible, but they felt they had lost the opportunity to talk about that because the company had been put in this position of being rather combative and sometimes abrasive. The idea was to say, 'We think we have programs in place and intentions to do good things that we should be out there talking about. But it means being a more open and accessible company.' "

Changing the Face of the Corporation.   In order to change their public image, a wide variety of communications initiatives were introduced. These changed the face of the corporation both within and without. The program included the following:

- A 24-hour toll-free media hot line to answer journalists' questions about Dow or anything to do with chemicals.
- Community Relations Resource Center, a resource base at Dow headquarters for the firm's community-relations personnel around the country. A wide variety of materials are available, from guidelines for working with local officials, to speeches, to prototypes of partnership programs with local schools.
- Management Speech Center, a support center created in an effort to bring Dow managers into various forums as speakers. The center helps train executives and coordinate decisions on audiences, locations, and speech content. "One of the things Dow's research indicated," says Olszewski, "was that the more that people had a one-on-one encounter with Dow people, especially management, the more they were inclined to have a favorable opinion of the company. So the speech center was one effort along those lines."
- Visible Scientist Program, developed with the realization that scientists have more credibility than managers or communications specialists with the public. About 15 scientists are trained annually to appear on talk shows and in front of citizens groups and newspaper editorial-board briefings around the country. Subjects discussed are those of concern to the general public, primarily safety and the environment.
- Two annual public interest reports, which cover Dow's efforts in the areas of environment, health and safety, community affairs, education, and opportunities for minorities and women. About 60,000 copies of the reports were sent out. That information has since been incorporated into Dow's annual reports.
- Adoption of a social cause, in the form of a partnership with the American Council on Transplantation. Dow gave significant financial support for a publicity campaign to educate the public on the

importance of organ donation, a cause intentionally chosen because it is unrelated to Dow business interests.

- Science Journalism Center at the University of Missouri, partially funded by Dow, to help train aspiring journalists to report scientific developments and improve the quality of science journalism.

- A crisis communications plan—something Dow realized no chemical company should be without. Dow made its crisis management programs more systematic and uniform across the company, ensuring regular review and practice.

- Advocacy Group Outreach, which has led to joint efforts with environmental organizations, such as the National Wildlife Federation, and other citizens groups, such as the League of Women Voters.

- A corporate advertising campaign, showing different ways in which Dow benefits society.

Grass-roots Communications.   In addition to these corporate initiatives, Dow has instituted several programs at the local level to open communications with the communities in which it operates. One such program is the company's plant tours. Although these had been available for many years in Dow communities around the world, the tours became a formalized program in the mid-1980s.

"We have thousands and thousands of people going through our plant locations on public tours," says Newman, "and environmental services is one area that's always requested. People always want to go in and see where we're treating waste water and see where our incinerator is and hear about how we manage the waste that is a result of operating a plant."

Community advisory panels serve as another useful forum for communicating with local citizens. The panels, which were created several years ago, meet on a regular basis and raise issues of all types having to do with Dow practices. Environmental matters are often the main focus, but other concerns, such as hiring practices and local purchasing policy, are also discussed. "That's one thing that's helped keep us aware of what's on the minds of the people in plant communities," says Newman. "And we recognize that we can't be preaching to them. We have to listen to what they want to say."

The composition of the panels lends them legitimacy and credibility with the community. Dow selects a core group of people and then lets them choose their fellow members.

"On our panel in Midland," says Newman, "we have a veterinarian and an obstetrician-gynecologist, the superintendent of schools, a student from the high school, and someone from the sheriff's department—it's a real cross section of people. Technically, they come not really representing their constituency or their business, but the community at large. But certainly their perspective comes from their professional background. People know them, people stop them in the grocery store

and say, 'I heard you're on the Dow committee; why don't you get them
to do this or that?' I think that being visibly known is a good way for
them to also get other input from their community members."

Each group works with a professional facilitator, chosen from outside
Dow, whose function is to get the meeting rolling and keep
communications flowing. "He doesn't have a Dow agenda in mind,"
Newman says. "He's just there to make sure that people's ideas get on
the table. Only one representative from Dow is in the room. This person
is there to listen and answer questions or bring in management to
answer the questions of the panelists."

At the heart of many of Dow's public affairs projects is employee
involvement. "Much of the outreach that we do is very personal," says
Newman, "and it goes back to our 62,000 employees. We work at getting
those people out to tell our story. First you have to empower your
employees, then let them go out and build relationships and help run
programs and work on task forces. They also escort environmental
groups on tours and speak to rotary clubs. The whole business of public
affairs is relationship building."

Working with the Watchdogs.   Dow's open approach to concerned
citizens applies also to organized special-interest groups, such as
environmental organizations. Newman says that it was dialogue with
some of Dow's critics that led the company to formalize its acclaimed
WRAP (Waste Reduction Always Pays) program. "It was really the
outgrowth of a couple of people who challenged us on waste reduction
and said, 'Show me the data. You say you're reducing waste, but can you
put it in black and white for me?' So we worked hard to get our internal
act together and put together a better internal auditing system for
keeping track of waste coming out of our plants and how much we were
reducing so we could provide this data to these people.

"We want to work with all sorts of groups," says Newman. "We want to
know what's on their minds, see if we can't compromise and work
together cooperatively with industry, academia, government, special-
interest groups—that's really the way you make progress in this country.
One company alone is not going to make enough of a difference to save
the environment. It has to be a collection of everyone, all of industry
and all of government and all of the special-interest groups working
together to come up with solutions. We try to get people from special-
interest groups onto our advisory panels. There are some people who
don't want to be a part of that, and that's worrisome because if they
don't want to even sit down and talk, if they just want to make
accusations, we really can't make much progress."

Dow is involved with environmental groups in other ways as well. For
instance, the company's director of environmental affairs spoke at a
regional Sierra Club meeting in Texas in January 1991, at the club's
request. "They said they wanted someone from management to talk
about what we're doing to protect the environment," says Newman.

"We're frequently doing things like that. We've met with the Audubon Society and with Sierra Club members out in California, where we have plants. At the local level we have a lot of Dow employees who are members of all kinds of environmental groups."

Dow seems to have found that working *with* government regulators and legislators rather than consistently against them is the smarter way to get things done.

"We have testified before congressional hearings on waste reduction," says Newman. "We appreciate opportunities to do that because it's a way for us to get our message before them on what we think is possible for us."

"I think the key is to be involved at an early stage with people who are drafting legislation," says Newman. "We have done that. Waste reduction is a good example. Representative Howard Wolpe [D-Mich.] introduced the waste-reduction bill, and in the drafting stage, he initiated contact with Dow. Some of his staffers came to see what is actually feasible in terms of waste reduction inside a chemical plant. It's one thing to sit in Washington and write the legislation; it's another to implement it. Sometimes, the two don't go hand in hand. Therefore, the ideal situation is to be involved up front in the drafting."

Nevertheless, Dow does not always support bills on the environment. Therefore, the difficult role the company must play is to lobby against an environmental bill and still maintain its image of being concerned about the environment. However, Newman believes that "Environmental issues are not black and white. There's so much gray area. On the surface it may seem that being against some bill that's supposed to protect the environment is bad. However, if we can talk it through, many times they'll find that it's the way that it's being proposed that we have problems with. Hopefully, we can compromise. There are always two sides of a story."

Environmental Events.   Dow also supports sponsorship of environment-related events, such as Earth Day 1990. Dow employees participated in company-backed activities that included planting trees and cleaning up highways.

In 1989, the company also helped organize and fund a cleanup of the trash that had accumulated on Mount Everest. A Dow employee who was also a mountain climber came to management with the idea. Comments Newman: "The project cleaned up Mount Everest and put a mechanism in place to keep it clean in the future. Furthermore, it gave off a message that we're concerned about the environment all over the world; and it was a neat way for one of our own employees to go out and practice environmentalism with company support. We got some good publicity, and we also did some internal publicity on our employees. That made everyone feel good."

"Great Things."   Probably the most visible of Dow's efforts is its corporate advertising campaign that centers around the line "Dow Lets You Do Great Things." The campaign was developed in the mid-1980s to increase public awareness of the company.

One of the more recent commercials focuses on plastics recycling. "Plastics are recyclable," says Newman, "and Dow is working to ensure that the message gets out there. A lot of people don't even realize that you can recycle plastic, so they jump on the bandwagon to ban plastics."

The campaign has a much wider purpose than just covering environmental issues, however.

"The environment was only one part of why their image was the way it was when we started the 'Great Things' campaign," says Wally Gaer, vice president and account supervisor at DMB&B, Dow's advertising agency. "There were a lot of problems, not the least of which was their role during the Vietnam War. Those things seemed to have a lot more impact than the fact that they were a chemical company."

The effects of the campaign have been positive, but slow in coming. "Changing public opinion toward companies tends to be glacial," says Dick Dalton, Dow's manager of corporate advertising. "It takes a long time to erase old images and establish new ones unless you have a revolutionary product introduction or something." Testing of attitudes before and after the campaign began showed a small but noticeable improvement in public attitudes toward Dow. "We've seen a gradual increase in favorability for the company," says Dalton.

He cautions, however, that the change cannot necessarily be attributed to the communications efforts alone. Performance in the financial markets has a large impact on people's perceptions of certain companies, too.

"Generally speaking, if the industry is not doing well, Dow is not doing well either," he explains. "However, we do rate well above the average for the chemical industry. In 1990, the industry took a nosedive in its public ratings, but Dow was able to maintain some strength. Overall, we are satisfied with the results that we're getting, although there's still room for improvement. But even if nothing had happened in terms of measurement, it would have been worth doing because of its effect on employee morale—that's probably worth a half a point of productivity right there."

Deeds to Back Up the Words.   Dow realizes that just showing pretty pictures and shaking a few hands is not enough. The whole communications effort would backfire if it did not have the substance to back up its claims. "I can't do my job unless we have our company act together," says Newman. "The performance certainly has to be there. We really work hard to try to communicate with substance so that we're not accused of greenwashing—everyone is very quick today to accuse you of greenwashing if you appear to be talking too much about your environmental performance. I'm always challenging our employees, 'Give me the data about how much we've reduced waste'—that's what people want to know; they want to see the curves. They want to know how much we've reduced in pounds, in tons. It's nice to talk about it but we need to show the data, the concrete evidence."

Olszewski agrees: "I think at the heart of all this, there really had to be substance. There really had to be a track record on environmental areas that was solid. I think we all agreed that if there wasn't, no amount of money spent on public relations would ever cover up that fact. Sooner or later, if it's just words, people discover that and then it all collapses and you're in worse shape than when you started.

"If you look at Dow's history from 1984 to now, it is a case of continually doing a better job of opening up the company and telling its good story of environmental matters. Dow made such a credible case that in 1989 it won the World Environment Center gold medal for international environmental achievement. That was one of the major successes. To me, it underscored the fact that there has been substance underneath the communications. In addition to that, Dow has taken on a reputation as being a leader in the whole waste-reduction area. When you ask most people in Washington who they think of when they think of corporate leaders in that area, Dow would have to be among the top three that most people name, if not the top one."

A Global Message?   Dow's approach to environmental issues is generally the same around the world. A new position, that of vice president of environmental health and safety, was created in 1990 to ensure that the waste-reduction and public-outreach programs are carried out globally.

Most of Dow's corporate communications program is not in place in other parts of the world. The "Great Things" advertising campaign, for example, is run only in the United States. "They don't necessarily translate," says Gaer, "because we have come to understand that Dow is not facing the same issues in Europe that it's facing in the United States. There isn't any holdover from the Vietnam War. That's not an issue there. We do think there's a role for an image campaign in the rest of the world. But if Dow's managers overseas view their image as a problem, they view it as something different."

Dalton, however, doesn't agree that the relevant issues are so different, and believes Dow should be doing a global ad campaign. "Personally, I don't think Dow's image problems on the environment are different internationally. Are we addressing them with corporate advertising? No. Why? The only reason I can see is that we're a very decentralized company; so there's nobody in Midland, for example, to tell people in Europe or South America or the Pacific Rim that they have to do corporate advertising." As a result, Dalton admits, a unified global image "doesn't exist for Dow, at least not through advertising."

Far from Finished.   Even in the United States, Dow has plenty of work ahead of it to improve and sustain its image. Says Newman, "There are a lot of people who don't believe the industry is going to change very much. There are people who, no matter what you do, will be skeptical toward you. Hopefully, there will always be people who challenge us also."

"We are very concerned with all the rhetoric that's going on now," says Charles Infante, manager of special projects, "in terms of the toxic substances produced by industries and in terms of the generation of products that need to be recycled and disposed of.

"But we are convinced that chemicals are essential. Chemistry is the backbone of a lot of technical development and has brought many of the things that we have that we take for granted. We want to be seen as a company that is sensitive to the concerns that people have with chemistry and chemicals. We want people to become more aware and technically literate so that they can see that 'chemistry' and 'chemicals' are not dirty words."

To keep up the momentum, Dow plans to stay its course and add new programs. "We, as a company, certainly recognize we have to put our money where our mouth is and really do substantial things, not just PR types of things to try to change our image," says Newman. "We know that we can't just give money to this or that cause. We need to show how our management is committed from the top to environmental protection, show how we're working in terms of reducing waste from a data standpoint.

"We're really going to concentrate on the basics, that is, operating our company in a safe and sound manner environmentally, and making sure that our plants are not emitting more than they should and working to reduce emissions from our plants," says Newman.

"We are looking for new ways to do things. For example, environmental education is one area we're examining very closely to see what we might be able to do to help work with schoolteachers and children in the area of conservation and recycling.

"Waste reduction will continue to be a very high priority," she continues. "The more you reduce waste, the less you have to recycle it or reuse it or incinerate it or treat it or landfill it. So we're trying to come up with innovative ideas on a monthly basis to reduce the amount of waste that we generate."

Dow's Vietnam legacy, though fading, will probably be around for a while. "It's dissipating," says Newman, "in that there are fewer people who bring it up just in terms of media and public calls.

"We see fewer people asking about it today than we did years ago. But we do recognize that a lot of people who lived through the Vietnam era—protestors, people who were in the war—are now in management, in decision-making positions, or in the media or the government," she observes. "It will be in some people's minds probably for another generation. All you can do is try to operate in an ethical and sound manner and try to overcome prejudices some people may have about the past. However, people still ask about it, and what I usually say is, 'Look at what Dow is doing today. Let me tell you about our plastics recycling and waste reduction and our conservation programs.' Hopefully, people will judge us on *all* that we do."

Case Example

Johnson & Johnson: Aiming for the Top*

1993 has become an important year in Europe, symbolizing the beginning of the EC internal market. For U.S. health-care products company Johnson & Johnson (J&J), 1993 also has symbolic importance. That year will mark an important milestone in the company's ambitious five-year Community Environmental Responsibility program. Launched in August 1988, the program aims to make J&J a global pacesetter in responsible environmental performance.

J&J's basic commitment to environmental management was set out in its Credo some 43 years ago. This stated: "We are responsible to the communities in which we live and work and to the world community as well . . . We must maintain in good order the property that we are privileged to use, protecting the environment and natural resources."

While the Credo provided the philosophical basis for J&J's Environmental Responsibility program, introduction of the U.S. community right-to-know (Sara Title III) legislation and related environmental initiatives indicated to management that a new emphasis had to be placed on preventive environmental action. First, J&J companies had to be made aware of legislation and corporate directives on the environment.

Second, it was determined to encourage a proactive approach to environmental matters. This has close links with J&J's quality improvement process: "Responsible management of the environment requires a continuous process of improvement."

Like the quality program, the environmental leadership initiative will affect "all areas of our business, from process to product, packaging to marketing," with the ultimate aim of "preventing the release of toxic or hazardous substances into the environment."

Four-Phase Environmental Management.   To support the Credo, the following four-phase program was developed.

Phase One: Training and Preparedness.   The goals of the first phase were relatively modest: to make all J&J facilities aware of the fundamental importance of regulatory compliance and of the need to participate in environmental activities in their communities. A corporate program reflecting J&J's decentralized management structure was developed and then customized at each facility. Because many of J&J's facilities have to handle chemicals, the company chose to focus on the subject of emergency response as a way of promoting the wider debate on environmental improvement.

Two tools were developed to guide and support the facilities:

---

* This section has been reprinted from the BI research report, *The Greening of Europe*, 1990.

- *Chemical communications handbook.* By helping to translate technical data into easily understood facts about compliance and safety, this handbook enables each facility to communicate effectively with outside interests.
- *Facility incident manual.* Designed as a comprehensive guide for use by facility emergency management personnel, the manual provides information on how to respond in the event of an incident and on how best to minimize its environmental, human, and capital impact.

To get Phase One started, an environmental assessment of J&J's facilities was used to gather background information. This was designed to help each facility identify emergency response capabilities and

---

Environmental Responsibility Program

Phase One: Training and Preparedness. Facilities to be made aware of legislation and corporate directives on the environment. Training in emergency response, communications, and compliance to ensure a complete state of readiness at each J&J work site.

Phase Two: Proactive Leadership Commitment. Development and implementation of an environmental strategy plan, with technical, employee, and community communication components for each facility.

Phase Three: The Marketplace. Evaluation of the impact of products and packaging to ensure environmental neutrality. Steps would include the following:

- Identify recyclable materials for ease of sorting by embossing or labeling with appropriate recycling symbols.
- Use printing inks that do not contain heavy metals.
- Use recycled plastics and paper fiber in products and packaging whenever possible.
- Implement product/process development policy which focuses on reducing impact at the earliest point in product and packaging design.

Phase Four: The Community. Participation in public/community programs, which could involve contributing expertise, funding, or sponsoring.

determine information requirements in order to develop a communications strategy.

A management training exercise was then scheduled to explain the purpose of the leadership program. Each three-day training session provided managers with the chemical communications handbook, the facility incident manual, and information on setting up a computerized emergency planning and response system at their site. Included was a crisis simulation session; role playing emphasized the importance of preparedness for incidents involving hazardous substances.

Phase Two: Proactive Leadership Commitment. Phase Two focused on the environmental program at each site. Its main objective was the development of a site-specific environmental strategic plan. The development and implementation of this plan involved challenges on three fronts: technical, community, and employee.

- *The technical challenge.* Continual assessment of operations, products, and packaging is stressed, along with an ongoing commitment to take actions to minimize their effect on the environment in order to reach the interim goal of neutral environmental impact.
- *The community challenge.* This focuses on communicating J&J's goal of environmental leadership by taking a proactive stand on all environmental issues through open, positive relationships with members of the communities in which it operates.
- *The employee challenge.* This is directed toward the implementation of employee communications and related programs that encourage employee support and participation in establishing J&J as an industry leader in community environmental safety.

Phase Three: The Marketplace. The third phase deals with products and their packaging, with the aim of minimizing their environmental impact, as well as reducing environmental impact at the source.

Environmental Leadership

- *Producer.* Pursue a goal of neutral environmental impact for all products, packaging, processes, and materials consistent with sound business practice.
- *User.* Educate the user in the disposal of all products, through packaging instruction and other appropriate means, which become a hallmark of environmental leadership and concern.
- *Proactive regulatory strategy.* Pursue a realistic legislation aggressively, consistent with Credo, policy, and leadership initiatives.

In the area of existing products and processes, the focus is on minimizing packaging and maximizing the use of recyclable and recycled materials. The use of nontoxic materials in all aspects of product containers and packaging is stressed.

A product/process development policy requires an environmental impact assessment of all new research and development projects. This procedure addresses raw materials, processing, packaging, and final product to ensure minimal environmental impact or, ideally, environmental neutrality.

Phase Four: The Community.   The fourth phase was concerned with public/community programs. These can range in scope from the corporate to the facility level. They include J&J's contributing expertise and/or funding in selected environmental projects, sponsoring/participating in national and local events, and active participation in environmentally responsible industry and academic organizations.

Vision and Realism.   J&J's Environmental Responsibility Program (see box, p. 101) combines two features essential to the success of a corporate environmental program: vision and realism. Without a long-term vision, such as J&J's to achieve "neutral environmental impact," companies will find themselves buffeted by the constantly changing expectations of regulators, employees, customers, and communities.

A vision sets the course, but it must be placed in the context of the realities of business if it is to have any impact on actual practice. Thus J&J recognizes the "pragmatic reality" that "some toxic or hazardous substances will be released into the environment." This puts the vision into perspective, so that while J&J acknowledges that some leakage will be inevitable, it must be "sufficiently small as to have no detectable long-term effect." By responding in a strategic fashion, J&J expects not only to protect its existing position, but also to unlock new opportunities.

There is now ample evidence to construct a whole series of environmental doomsday scenarios. Global warming alone raises the prospect of a far-reaching ecological catastrophe. For companies, the competitive pressures of the marketplace have often been an excuse for sidelining environmental considerations. It is unlikely that such an approach will be viable in the future.

Business-as-usual attitudes toward environmental protection have already become a commercial liability in a world where expectations are constantly rising. A new "green" competitive advantage is emerging among those companies that have accepted the need to change course ahead of legislation. The successful companies of the 1990s will certainly be those that adopt the goal of environmental leadership.

8

Issue Management and a Strategic Global Vision

With the diversity of issues that are important to any global company, developing a reasonable early-warning system for tracking developments that can negatively affect a company's image is crucial. The idea is to identify potential problems before they develop so that the company has an opportunity to shape, rather than react to, public comment and decision making.

What is *not* needed for successful issue management is the collection of more information of the kind that most companies already receive on an ongoing basis. More useful is a systematized tracking system that establishes what information must be gathered, by whom, how it is to be obtained, and what should be done with it.

Management of an Issue

As part of its image strategy, a company must develop a response mechanism for dealing with public policy issues. These are broadly defined as external factors about which a company must take a position, make a statement, take an action, or modify the manner in which business is conducted. They include situations, questions, occurrences, events, or differences of opinion that are or may be embodied in a law or public policy.

There are many different ways for companies to stay on top of "public good" issues that present areas of potential threat or opportunity. The best approach is to identify a concern in the incipient stages of its life cycle—while it is still of only passing interest to the public. If a problem is not dealt with until it has reached crisis proportions, a company's ability to influence the public's perception will be greatly minimized.

Monitoring Issues

Even if an issue management system is not overly formal, developing it can still seem fairly overwhelming. The first attempt at identifying the issues to be tracked may produce upward of 100 concerns that could affect the global company. Since no company can effectively track so many issues simultaneously, the list should be narrowed down to the 10 that are most important. These should then be followed systematically (a sample issue management worksheet is at the end of this chapter). In following these issues, others that may be of importance to the company will also emerge.

The following is a useful program to develop for issue tracking:

1. Scan selected publications, including

   - General press
   - Specialized industry and business newsletters and reports
   - Industry opponents' publications
   - Data banks, library services
   - Government documents

2. Establish a filing system to organize information so that the most important issues in specific countries or regions are identified. Global issues (those with the potential for affecting all people or nations in which a company does business) should be kept by subject category, not country category.

3. Maintain contacts with interested outsiders, such as

   - Government officials and politicians
   - U.S. embassy personnel
   - Sympathetic special-interest groups and their lobbyists (e.g., industry and business associations, professional groups)
   - Researchers and academics
   - Journalists
   - Consultants
   - Customers
   - Suppliers

4. Actively solicit and share information

   ■ Internally with affiliate personnel at local headquarters, in the field and at corporate headquarters

   ■ With allies in other companies, trade associations, the professions

5. Consolidate what is learned during routine business discussions and during preparations of plans or reports. This is usually accomplished by a committee that includes top management and others affected by the issue. Based on input from those who would be involved in implementing the organization's response, position papers and plans are developed by staff subject to the approval of senior management.

6. Conduct an annual review of potential issues. This permits a broader overview, making it possible to identify priority issues for the following year. An ideal time for this process is when the strategic plan is being prepared. Bear in mind that evaluation—the final step in the issues management process—helps determine the effectiveness and impact of the program. Evaluation should help to establish how long the program continues or whether changes or adjustments need to be made.

Developing a Response

If a company is required to develop a public response to an issue or problem, management should be sure to examine the following areas:

■ *Critical publics.* Identify people (i.e., customers, employees, anyone affected by corporate policy or products), pressure groups, lobbies and address them in the release.

■ *Components for escalation.* Recognize the wronged parties and address how the problems will be corrected, bearing in mind the public-interest potential of the announcement.

■ *Potential constituency.* Organize those who will benefit from change, develop third-party allies, sensitize the media, particularly if an action program is developed to address an issue.

■ *Focus on a target.* Define the "bad guys," evaluate corporate vulnerability, develop strategy to deal with detractors.

■ *Begin a dialogue.* Make high-level contact with corporation(s) in similar straits, jointly establish credibility with the skeptics.

■ *Lock into the media.* Sell the issue, play responses, expand constituency, and intensify pressure to get the corporate viewpoint across.

- *Negotiate terms.*   Consider what corporate changes would satisfy critics.
- *Communicate victory.*   Establish how the public and, therefore, the company will benefit.

Issue Management Matrix

The following is a list of key external and internal factors that can have measurable impact on corporate performance as well as image. These factors impact both relationships with local constituencies as well as overall profitability. Tracking them will help a company identify specific public policy issues in countries where the company does business. The list may also be used as the basis for creating a filing system for issue tracking.

1. *External Issue Factors*
    - Government Economic Policies
      Budget/tax regulations
      Productivity supports
      Trade politics/export incentives (see #4)
    - Employment Incentives
    - Demographic Trends and Birthrates
    - Mortality Factors
    - Attitudes Toward Social Change
      Support for innovation
      R&D support policies
      Decentralization/urban rural policies
      Restrictions on media/cultural expression
2. *Attitudes toward Corporate Social Performance*
    - Corporate Governance Rules
    - Disclosure of Public Information
    - Policies
      Environmental hazards
      Business plan details
      Financial data
    - Regulation of Transborder Data Flows
    - Pressure Group Activists
    - Attitudes of Local Enterprise
    - Contribution Trends (i.e., philanthropy)

3. *Employee Relations*
   - Relations with Organized Labor/Unions
   - Disclosure Rules
   - Privacy Protection
   - Employment Protection—Individual and Collective
   - Sexual, Racial, Religious, or Age Discrimination or Harassment
   - Protection for Whistle Blowers
   - Retirement Benefits
   - Career Development
   - Training/Retraining
   - Compensation Practices, Including Protection of Income
   - Occupational Health and Safety
   - Effect of Changing Work Values
     Management style
     Motivation/communications/job satisfaction
     Retirement/training/development
     Compensation and benefit packages
     Productivity
   - Local and Minority Employment

4. *Trade and Investment Regulations*
   - Accounting/Reporting Standards
   - Ownership Restrictions
   - Export Performance (company's balance of payments)
   - Development Goals, Industrialization Priorities
   - Restrictive Business Practices/Technology Transfer
   - Employment Practices
   - Investment Laws
   - National Treatment of Corporations
   - Import Restrictions
   - Boycott Rules
   - Positions on Multilateral Trade Negotiations
   - Extraterritorial Application of U.S. Law (i.e., Foreign Corrupt Practices Act, antitrust law)
   - Trade and Export Incentives
   - Protectionism/Economic Nationalism
   - International Financing/Debt

5. *Product Standards*

- Product Effectiveness
- Product Safety
  Liability
  Health-risk ingredients
  Bans
  Inspections
- Labeling Requirements
- Packaging
  Disposal
  Tamper resistance
  Childproofing vs. needs of the elderly
- Consumer Protection
  Watchdog groups (law, stockholders, media)
  Warranty standards
  Disclosure to consumers
  Product liability rules
- Pricing Practices
- Marketing and Advertising
  Restrictive practices (advertising, promotion)
  Food marketing
- Patent and Trademark Protection
  Gray-market goods
  Criteria for determining abuse of patent rights
  Compulsory licensing

Key Organizations

The following is a compilation of key organizations developed by a global pharmaceutical company to monitor its own issues. All MNCs would benefit by having a similar list applicable to specific industries.

Public/Government Organizations

United Nations (UN)
International Labor Organization (ILO)
UN Conference on Trade and Development (UNCTAD)
UN Center on Transnational Corporations (UNCTC)
UN Industrial Development Organization (UNIDO)

World Industrial Property Organization (WIPO)
World Health Organization (WHO)
UN Children's Fund (UNICEF)
Other UN agencies

Pressure Groups

Health Action International (HAI)
International Organization of Consumer Unions (IOCU)
Medical Lobby for Appropriate Marketing (Malam)

Trade Professional Associations/Business Services

Manufacturers associations
Proprietary associations
Chamber of commerce
National associations of manufacturers
Advertising associations
Retailers associations
Business services/consultants

Professional Associations and Organizations

Issue Management Worksheet

This issue management worksheet, developed by a global company, is a suggested framework for tracking issues.

Issue: _____

Management responsibility for issue: _____

Other departments that need to be consulted/informed:

■ Affiliate: _____

_____

■ Region: _____

_____

■ Group: _____

_____

■ Operations: _____

_____

■ Corporate: _____

Spokespersons:
■ Calls: _____

_____

■ Letters: _____

Why is this issue important?
■ Short term: _____

_____

■ Long term: _____

_____

Who are the key proponents and what are their agendas and strategies?

_____

_____

Who are the key adversaries and what are their agendas and strategies (if different from proponents)?

_____

_____

What are the views of key publics on this issue and how is our position perceived?

- General public: _____

_____

- Media: _____

_____

- Executive branch of government: _____

_____

- Legislative branch of government: _____

_____

- Industry: _____

_____

- Potential allies: _____

_____

- Employees: _____

_____

- Local community: _____

_____

- Customers: _____

_____

Is regulatory/legislative action likely? _____

Rated as high—medium—low, what is our vulnerability to:

- Negative publicity? _____
- Significant lawsuits? _____
- Employee morale problems? _____

- Customer backlash? _____
- Financial community backlash? _____
- Security concerns? _____
- Product recall/ban? _____
- Other? _____

What is our position? _____

_____

_____

Is there a need to prepare a position paper? _____

If yes, by whom and when? _____

_____

What are our
- Strengths? _____
- Weaknesses? _____

What approaches can the company take to
- Defuse issue? _____

_____

- Turn it into an opportunity? _____

_____

- Seek a compromise? _____

_____

- Obtain support of allies? _____

_____

What specific actions will be taken? _____

_____

9
Preserving Your Image

Almost every company has had to deal with at least one crisis at some point in its history. It may be a food company that inadvertently sells tainted food, a chemical manufacturer that spills toxins into a local river, an automaker whose vehicle is found to be unsafe, or a company in any industry that is caught making false product claims. In all cases, the management agenda should be to take responsibility, to provide accurate information, to rectify the problem, and to restore the company's business and reputation as quickly as possible.

Crisis Management

According to Raymond O'Rourke, executive vice president of crisis communications at Burson-Marsteller, a worldwide communications and consulting firm, many companies continue to "get it wrong" when handling a crisis. This does not surprise him, for he does not think there is a specific formula or learning curve that executives can follow. Companies can and should create a crisis management team of key executives and develop contingency plans for crises they can anticipate, those relating directly to the nature of their business (e.g., oil spills or chemical fires). But O'Rourke maintains that in a global company many problems cannot be foreseen.

"Every crisis, when it breaks, is a unique situation," he says. "Unfortunately, most of the lessons that a company learns come during its handling of the crisis—and emergency decisions are not based on hindsight. The facts on which a correct judgment can be made are not available at the time a crisis erupts or unfolds. It takes time to muddle through the reality of the situation."

When disaster strikes, adds O'Rourke, perhaps the best thing a company can have on its side is a favorable image. "Where you end up depends on where you start from," he says. "If you have a good reputation with all your key audiences, and if you're known for quality, reliability, and responsiveness, it will be infinitely easier to put a crisis behind you than if you're unknown or perceived negatively to begin with. There's no question in my mind that a smart, ongoing public relations effort will build a bank of goodwill you can draw from later."

In a global marketplace, thanks to advanced communications technologies, news travels fast—and bad news travels very fast. A crisis affecting a company, especially a well-known MNC—regardless of location or magnitude—can in a matter of hours taint the image a company has cultivated carefully over years. For a firm operating in many countries, a problem at any of its operations is usually an immediate headache for corporate headquarters. "The explosion in global communications definitely complicates the crisis management process," observes O'Rourke.

Not only is the global grapevine almost instantaneous, it is highly sophisticated. The media have become powerful players in a crisis, not merely chroniclers. "Journalists today don't just report the crisis, they also write about how management is dealing or not dealing with the problems at hand," O'Rourke notes.

Because of more aggressive media reporting and the public's heightened expectations of a company involved in the crisis, many experts believe that some choices are no longer open to CEOs. For example, the CEO is now expected to be at the scene of the emergency. Although from a management or operational perspective it may not make the best sense to have the CEO on the scene, O'Rourke believes that "since *Valdez*, it's not a battle worth fighting. It's unwinnable. The media, and therefore the public, expect the CEO to be at the scene."

He says that cultural differences and attitudes must be considered when handling a corporate problem with potential image-damaging implications. O'Rourke cites the incident in 1990 when Perrier bottles were taken off supermarket shelves because benzene was discovered in the water.

"The Perrier recall was initiated in the United States," says O'Rourke. "The French felt that the Americans were grossly overreacting. They didn't understand why this product should be recalled because of a virtually unmeasurable quantity of benzene." This attitude did not represent an unwillingness by management to face up to the problem; rather, it reflected a basic cultural difference. As O'Rourke explains, "The French drink bottled water for what's in it—the minerals. Americans, on the other hand, drink bottled water for what's *not* in it—the pollutants. So when you tell a Frenchman there's something in his Perrier besides minerals, you get a Gallic shrug. In the United States, though, the usual reaction is that the product must be impure, it shouldn't be on the shelf, it's a health hazard, and so on."

Such cultural differences make it much more difficult for an MNC to resolve a crisis than for a company operating in a single market or in several markets with similar cultures. In the end, Perrier solved its problem through bilateral cooperation: The production process in France was changed to remove any possibility of benzene entering the water, and the president of Perrier's U.S. subsidiary worked closely with the parent company's CEO to deal with the initial negative publicity and, later, the remarketing of the "new" Perrier water.

Given all these complexities, is there any way a company can tell whether it is handling an emergency well? Yes, say the experts. The CEO and the crisis management team should establish at the outset what they believe will constitute a successful resolution of the emergency. That way, when the media, competitors, and others second-guess the company's decisions, the management team will itself know what a satisfactory outcome is. "Unless you clearly identify your objective, you may be held to an unrealistically high standard," says O'Rourke.

Developing a Crisis Communications Plan

Despite the substantial resources global companies devote to building a positive image, a single piece of bad news can seriously disrupt relations with customers, shareholders, governments, the financial community, and the media. Indeed, selling products, attracting capital, impressing investors, and recruiting employees are all difficult if the company is a major polluter, has been involved in cheating on government contracts, or has given the public reason to believe it has no credibility.

Many firms have determined that crisis communications planning will minimize the damage to a company's reputation when a crisis erupts. They are devising specific strategies to help them reach their key constituencies in times of corporate distress. The following checklist is based on the experiences of a number of MNCs that have gone through crises of one sort or another.

What to Do . . .

- *Define the scope of a likely crisis.* Analyzing the impact of hypothetical events on the company can help avoid a major pitfall in crisis management: the tendency to overreact to bad news. An exaggerated response can be just as dangerous as a dilatory or insufficient one; it will fuel rather than contain the public relations "fire." Global managers need to ask whether the problem is likely to have worldwide and companywide ramifications, or whether its effects will be limited to a single community or country. Is the problem best handled by local or regional managers, or should headquarters take control? Answers to these questions will help identify the type of communications effort needed to get your message across in a variety of situations.

■ *Consider the historical record.* Place the situation in perspective by examining how other global companies have handled similar crises in the past. Develop a file of case studies. One European multinational corporation uses such materials as a basis for "ranking" potential crises according to the level of severity, with appropriate action plans that can deal with each situation.

■ *Target your audience.* Crisis communications, like a marketing program, are most effective when tailored to specific audiences. Appeals to an undifferentiated mass of people are costly and can fan the flames of negative publicity. Companies should focus on two groups: those directly affected by the event and those who can help resolve it. For example, when confronted by a worldwide boycott by activists protesting its infant-formula promotional practices, Nestle SA of Switzerland responded by (1) shoring up its relationships with its customers, suppliers, and distributors, and (2) establishing a dialogue with religious groups, health-care professionals, and other influential intermediaries.

■ *Keep employees informed.* Failure to explain company actions to employees will hurt morale and hasten the spread of rumors. Loss of its internal constituency will, in turn, undermine management's efforts to retain the confidence of creditors, customers, and other outside constituencies.

■ *Centralize information flows.* By making a single person or staff unit responsible for communications, executives can control the dissemination of critical information and ensure that the company's message is clear and consistent. Officially designated spokespersons should be not only the sources of on-the-record information and quotes but also the providers of any background analysis or material the company wishes to supply. It is essential that all employees defer to the official source: The company must act and speak with one voice.

■ *Develop a clearance policy for company statements*—and disseminate it throughout the organization. Make sure everyone in significant management posts knows who must clear statements to the press and how to reach those individuals 24 hours a day. Such a procedure must be in place before a crisis occurs, because once events are unfolding rapidly and the press is clamoring for answers, it is too late. Putting reporters off while someone tries to find out who must clear the response will only lend credence to charges of indecisiveness or ducking the issue.

- *Choose spokespeople who can communicate effectively.* Many executives with public-liaison responsibilities have no training in communicating on television. This can easily be rectified by a few sessions with professional communications coaches available at most public relations agencies or specialized public-speaking firms.

  Some companies go even further: The Swiss pharmaceutical firm Ciba-Geigy has developed a cadre of media specialists selected not because of their years of experience in company affairs but because of their promotional skills and ability to project a pleasant image to TV viewers. This approach may well be the wave of the future, and it is certainly one no major company can afford to ignore.

  Yet another approach is to have the CEO or other senior executive be the spokesperson for the company. Some firms believe strongly that their credibility is enhanced when a top manager puts him- or herself directly on the firing line. This strategy worked well in the following J&J case. Although there is no rule of thumb, perhaps the best advice is that if the chairperson or president is a very quick study, does not get flustered under intense questioning, and presents a serious yet friendly image on TV, he or she can probably serve effectively as the company's chief spokesperson.

- *Report your own bad news.* By releasing damaging information as soon as you can confirm the details, the company reaps a number of benefits: It can defuse the impact of a news organization's "breaking" the story. It enhances corporate credibility and discourages speculative exposes. It provides the company with an early opportunity to give its own interpretation of the news and to provide background that may help put it in an appropriate context. Finally, having company executives play the role of informed commentator may also put some distance between the company and the crisis at hand.

- *Tell the truth.* Ethical considerations obviously apply here, but most MNCs adopt the approach for another reason as well: Honesty makes it easier to challenge inaccurate or biased media coverage. Executives must avoid the appearance of withholding facts—a terse "no comment" guarantees that any subsequent effort to present the facts will be greeted with skepticism. One notorious example of abysmal communications strategy: After the U.S. space shuttle *Challenger* with five astronauts aboard exploded into millions of pieces while the world watched their TVs in horror, the National Aeronautics and Space Administration said: "We fulfilled our disclosure obligation by confirming the shuttle exploded. We have no further comment."

■ *Update the crisis communications plan regularly.* Changes should reflect new products and services (as well as attendant areas of liability), acquisitions or investments in other sectors or countries, industry regulatory trends, and new developments in communications technology.

. . . And a Few What Not to Dos

■ *Avoid off-the-record interviews.* These almost always result in deviation from the company line by the person giving the interview and virtually guarantee misrepresentation by the reporter. Such interviews also raise the specter of favoritism in dealing with the press.

■ *Resist debating the issues with the press or corporate critics.* The emphasis should always be on action that the company is taking to relieve the crisis: assisting, negotiating, finding a solution.

■ *Never attempt to fix blame.* As key institutions of society, global companies are expected to act responsibly. Any attempt to lay the burden at someone else's door—however justified—is usually condemned by governments and the public as an attempt to shirk responsibility.

Case Example

How Johnson & Johnson Set the Standard

The Tylenol tampering tragedy that befell New Brunswick, New Jersey-based Johnson & Johnson (J&J) in the early 1980s has become a model for effective crisis management. It is the subject of a Harvard Business School case study, and the lessons learned from the incident are taught at all major business schools. The facts were simple: In 1982, seven people in the Chicago area died after taking Tylenol capsules that had been laced with cyanide by an anonymous criminal. Tylenol was at that time the leading pain-relief product in the United States, taken by some 100 million Americans. It was responsible for 13 percent of J&J's year-to-year sales growth and 33 percent of the company's profit growth. The brand held a 37 percent market share, outselling Anacin, Bayer aspirin, Bufferin, and Excedrin combined.

When the crisis struck, J&J had a highly significant fact in its favor: It was clearly not at fault, but had been victimized by an unknown poisoner. Occupying the moral high ground certainly helps a company throughout a crisis. Most companies caught up in disasters do not have that advantage (witness the tribulations of Exxon, responsible for the *Valdez* oil spill; Bon Vivant, whose botulism-tainted soup caused several deaths; and Firestone, whose defective tires resulted in auto accidents). Also helpful was J&J's generally positive public image: It was seen as a good company, tied together globally by the principles of its "caring" credo.

Still, the public relations challenge was considerable: People were dying from the firm's product; the company's stock was dropping. Within days, Tylenol's share of the analgesic market fell 87 percent.

On the advice of Burson-Marsteller, which guided the company throughout the crisis, J&J's CEO James Burke formed a seven-member strategy team within hours of the first news of the poisonings. The crisis task force met twice a day, made decisions as the facts unfolded, and coordinated all companywide actions. J&J immediately ordered the removal of all Tylenol bottles from stores across the nation and destroyed its entire stock of capsules.

To communicate directly and quickly with consumers, the company took a number of steps. It placed a full-page ad in major newspapers, giving the facts about the tragedy and offering customers an exchange of Tylenol capsules for tablets. It set up a special toll-free consumer hot line within a week to respond to inquiries regarding the safety of Tylenol. During the first week alone, 30,000 calls were logged—considerably more than anticipated, leading the crisis team to install 55 additional hot lines at its New Brunswick headquarters. Independent research organizations were hired to conduct daily surveys to track consumer awareness and public attitudes toward the crisis.

Press conferences and releases from headquarters resulted in 80,000 separate news stories in U.S. newspapers and hundreds of hours of national and local television coverage. Chairman Burke was the company spokesperson and made himself readily available to the media. He went on the popular Phil Donahue talk show and the investigative news program *60 Minutes*, known for its intense scrutiny of corporate America. Interviewer Mike Wallace stated that although Wall Street had been contemplating writing off the company, it was now "hedging its bets because of J&J's stunning campaign of facts, money, the media, and truth."

While few would say that J&J as a company is better off as a result of the Tylenol crisis, clearly little or nothing was lost in terms of image. The firm positioned itself as a champion of the consumer, defined the phrase "corporate responsibility," and established a standard of crisis communications by which other companies will be judged for years to come. Today J&J is usually asked by the media for comments when calamity strikes some other company.

Case Example

Elf Aquitaine: Handling an Oil Spill

On June 8, 1990, the French petroleum and chemicals producer Elf Aquitaine found himself facing a major industrial catastrophe: A

Norwegian supertanker, the *Mega Borg*, exploded, killing four crewmen and releasing 4.5 million gallons of flaming light crude oil into the Gulf of Mexico, 60 miles from Galveston, Texas. The oil in the tanker belonged to a Houston-based Elf subsidiary.

Elf's Paris-based top management team had watched with understandably keen interest as other oil companies grappled with the problems associated with oil spills and accidents in recent years. The Exxon *Valdez* and *Piper Alpha* cases were particularly instructive. (In the latter incident, an Occidental Petroleum drilling platform off the cost of Scotland blew up and killed 157 people.) One of the most important lessons Elf learned, according to Thomas Saunders, head of international relations at Elf's Paris headquarters, was that careful handling of communications not only can help resolve the actual problem but also can minimize the harm inflicted on a company's image.

Favorable Circumstances. Although any association with an environmental disaster is difficult for a company, Elf's task was made easier by circumstances considerably less daunting than those that accompanied the *Valdez* spill. For one thing, the oil never reached shore, because of Elf's containment efforts. In addition, weather conditions were favorable and flames burned off much of the slick, making the cleanup far less complicated than in the Exxon case.

"I'd say from the standpoint that the oil never really had an impact on the land, everybody came out reasonably well," says John Murphy, a vice president at the New York-based public relations agency Hill & Knowlton, which did a study on the crisis.

Most important, though, Elf had no legal liability for the spill: The shipper, not the cargo owner, was legally liable. This not only kept the company out of a huge legal entanglement like the one that confronted Exxon, but also lowered public expectations regarding Elf.

Despite the company's lack of legal liability, Elf's CEO, Loik Le Floch Prigent, decided the company should help with the cleanup. Thus, while the shipper dealt with the blazing vessel, Elf spent about $8 million on containing and cleaning up the spill. Enlisting the aid of two of its U.S. subsidiaries, it quickly located and hired a firm to provide oil skimmers and dispersants. In Elf's view, this prompt response was critical in keeping the slick from reaching shore.

A Low-Key PR Approach. Besides controlling the physical damage, Elf had to develop a public relations plan to ensure that word got out quickly and accurately about its response to the disaster. Within hours of the accident, communications specialists, fully briefed by top management, were on a plane to the United States. By that afternoon they were in Houston (about 45 miles from Galveston, the site of the spill), meeting with members of Elf's local management team to decide what to do and say.

Part of the challenge was the desire to adhere to the company's longstanding policy of keeping a low profile with the media. "There's always a danger of doing too much, of tooting your own horn too much," Saunders says. "But then you can't keep silent, either. Silence is not always golden, sometimes silence is guilt. We had to let people know what we were doing to rectify the situation without appearing self-serving."

The company put out one news release explaining its involvement and actions. Although Elf had someone available for comment, for the most part it did not actively seek publicity. The company's PR activities were aided by the U.S. Coast Guard's Public Information Assistance Team. This group centralizes communications in disaster situations in which the Coast Guard is involved, partly by meeting regularly with journalists. "We had a representative at all those meetings," Saunders explains. "The team also helped by letting the press know that someone from Elf was there. So although we were in Houston, not Galveston, we were quite available to speak to reporters."

To ensure a smooth ending to the crisis, Elf's crisis team stayed in Houston for two weeks, until the last of the remaining cargo of oil was safely transferred to another ship. Saunders notes, "Toward the end, there was much less need for PR efforts, but there was always the potential for something to go wrong. Plus, there were some follow-up stories being done, so we needed to stay until everything was finished and the potential danger was over."

Some Criticism, Some Praise.   Although all those involved in the incident came under some criticism, most was leveled at the shipping company, the U.S. Coast Guard, and, by extension, the U.S. government. Barbara Crews, mayor of Galveston, says, "The overall response was terribly slow, and the fault could be shared by many parties. There was insufficient enforcement of regulations, for which I blame the federal government."

However, even some tough environmental critics concede that Elf performed well. Brandt Mannchen, a member of the Coastal Affairs Committee of the Lone Star Chapter of the Sierra Club, makes this observation about Elf's voluntary cleanup effort: "I'm glad they did it. They might have been sued anyway, but I think it should be a corporate ethic: If you are involved in a situation like that, you should take responsibility for helping in the cleanup. If you don't get involved, you're likely to get a black eye from a PR standpoint anyway. I'd like to see this become a routine thing for other businesses, rather than engaging in all kinds of finger pointing."

From a communications viewpoint, the comments from the media were mostly positive. Saunders notes: "In Houston, they said that Elf was open, although a bit camera-shy, which was true. But they were quite satisfied with what we were doing, the fact that we were returning calls and answering questions and so forth. That was what they were interested in."

Other oil companies have studied the crisis and commended Elf's approach. "Some casual remarks were made to Elf employees that Elf had dealt with the situation correctly to the benefit of the whole industry," says Saunders. Says Rick Hagar, coordinator of media relations for American Petrofina, "They did a fine job. I can't say how we would have handled a spill like that because we've never been in that type of situation. But we did learn from it."

Hill & Knowlton's Murphy agrees that the overall outcome of the public relations effort was about as good as a company in that situation could hope for, given the tenuous line between too much press and not enough. "Elf Aquitaine is not a company that sells to the consuming public. So from that standpoint it doesn't necessarily need a great deal of public exposure. On the other hand, because it is a big company, it certainly wants the world to know that it is environmentally sensitive. I would say the company handled the balance extremely well in that regard. It wasn't necessarily given banner headlines because it came to the aid of the cleanup effort. On the other hand, it wasn't necessarily singled out, except in a few minor cases, as being the owner of the product."

Secrets of Success.   Elf found the following steps especially helpful in managing the situation and informing the public of its efforts to clean up the spill:

- *Maintain good press relations.*   "Previously, we had spoken with a lot of journalists about the Exxon *Valdez* and Occidental Petroleum accidents, and we tried to find out what was good and bad in the way press relations were handled," says Saunders. "What we found out was that Occidental was open and available to journalists. Exxon was just the opposite, and that's where its public relations problems began. We put a lot of emphasis on the local press. We felt they were important because it was in their backyard."

- *Have a plan.*   The crisis team found it useful to speak with people at two Elf subsidiaries in Norway and the United Kingdom. These subsidiaries have very detailed, specific crisis contingency programs that supplement the general crisis plan for the entire Elf group. Part of the training includes a crisis simulation exercise in which real reporters participate. They interview communications personnel and other crisis team members and then write mock stories. Each interviewee's response is evaluated and critiqued on the basis of the finished stories.

  Another part of the plan, which Saunders found particularly useful, was the expedient of enlisting "nonessential personnel" to assist in crisis communications. Saunders explains, "There are people in finance or in other departments who are not immediately needed to handle the emergency. These people are asked to double in communications so there is always someone available who can answer the phone and who can relay the information as quickly as possible."

In Houston, a crude-oil trader was pressed into temporary PR service and proved to be very helpful.

- *Involve top management.*   Decisive and supportive senior managers made the PR team's job easier. "Top management was a big help in that they made decisions quickly, were very clear, listened to the possibilities, and were available for communications purposes," recalls Saunders. "That's extremely important, because often people are so preoccupied with operations that they let communications fall by the wayside. The chairman himself agreed that should there be major pollution from the spill, he would certainly come to the United States to meet with government people and the press, which was reassuring."

- *Empower the PR people.*   While top management support is essential, too much centralized control can slow things down and muddle communications efforts. Guy E. Brown II, a principal in the Houston-based public relations agency Brown, Nelson & Associates, was a counselor for the shipowners in the incident. In a recent article he wrote for the *Public Relations Journal,* he stresses the importance of keeping PR managers well briefed about developments as they occur and giving these managers the authority to release pertinent information. Murphy echoes those concerns: "One of the first problems our clients find when running through crisis training exercises is a breakdown in the flow of communications from the crisis site to the communications center. Many executives don't anticipate the sheer volume of media inquiries that such a situation brings."

- *Provide backup in every port.*   Elf's support staff in Houston turned out to be invaluable. Saunders notes that local employees know the area better and are thus extremely helpful with logistics. "They are a tremendous help, even from the point of view of just providing secretarial services and that sort of thing," he says.

  Murphy adds that "a lot of companies are looking at points of entry—the locations where they are shipping their product—and the kinds of communications or crisis management capabilities they have in those areas. They're looking at those points where communication would become critical from the standpoint of the need for an instantaneous response."

- *Be prepared for all stages of media inquiry.*   Murphy asserts that there is a classic sequence of reporting that goes on with any kind of crisis: Phase I is the day the incident occurs. At that time, journalists concentrate on reporting the facts of the event and the background of the parties involved. For instance, if a ship is involved, the media will want to know its capacity, its port of call, its port of origin, its cargo, and so on. In the heat of the crisis, it is important to make sure company spokespeople have such details at their fingertips. By the second or third day, Phase II sets in, when the media examine recovery efforts, again in a very factual manner.

  Phase III is the analytical stage, the period when the company must be especially careful. "That's when it starts to become speculative," notes Murphy, "not necessarily on the part of reporters, but because they will seek expert testimony for the reasons behind the crisis. This can be fatal if the company's communications people don't have all the information, because the media will turn to other sources, such as academics, politicians, or unions. The risk is that you lose some control. And then it starts falling into attempts to lay blame for the incident or identify the perceived failures, either in causing the incident or in the recovery effort. It ultimately ends up with a speculation about who's liable for all this. Look at the way the media covered the *Mega Borg* spill. They started to raise serious questions about the entire effort when they perceived failures or when experts they had contacted started to raise questions about the failure of the recovery effort. But this really had to do with the time it took to get equipment into place. In any case, that was a criticism not of Elf Aquitaine but of the ship's owners."

- *Let outsiders defend you when possible.* Independent scientists and analysts are more credible in these situations than company spokespersons, so if there is good news to tell, let them tell it. For example, when tarballs washed up on Texas beaches, the Coast Guard analyzed them and announced that they had not come from the *Mega Borg*, but from another ship in the gulf. "I think the Coast Guard was extremely helpful because they spoke officially," comments Saunders. "If the owners of the *Mega Borg* had announced the news instead, nobody would have believed them."

- *Test the plan.* Brown, Nelson & Associates emphasizes the need to take the plan for a trial run. "Any crisis communications team— management, public relations staff, public relations counsel—should stress systematic review and testing of its emergency strategies and tactics before the red light flashes."

Case Example

Volvo: Weathering an Advertising Fiasco

Over many years, Volvo of Sweden has built a reputation for the quality, dependability, and safety of the autos it manufactures; Volvos are widely considered among the world's safest cars. With 80 percent of its sales coming from outside its home country, Volvo is in many respects a global company (even though its management and board of directors are solidly Swedish).

The perception of the Volvo station wagon as a safe car is grounded in reality. In 1990, the U.S. Highway Loss Data Institute rated it number one in terms of safety, compared with U.S., Japanese, and other European cars. Nearly every auto manufacturer has adopted Volvo's "safety cage" design, introduced in 1944, which reinforces the car's passenger compartment with steel sections along the roof, door pillars, and side rocker panels.

In light of its genuine concern with safety and its carefully cultivated global image stressing safety, Volvo's recent crisis over a mishandled ad was particularly embarrassing. The misrepresentation that was the centerpiece of the ad directly called into question the company's well-honed and well-protected reputation.

Management's response went a long way toward preventing worldwide damage to Volvo's image—although its success is hard to measure. In any case, it is clear that the company's credibility was sustained by a stellar reputation built over the past several decades. A company without such a deep reservoir of good public opinion would almost certainly have fared much worse than did Volvo.

The Ad in Question.   At end-1990, Volvo unveiled a striking new print and TV ad campaign depicting a car-crushing exhibition held the previous June in Austin, Texas. In the ad, when a "monster truck"—a giant pickup with huge tires, named *Bear Foot*—runs over a row of cars, all are flattened except a Volvo station wagon. The popular national U.S. newspaper *USA Today* published an article singling out the ad as one of the most effective television promotions for 1991 model-year cars—going so far as to call it "the best of the best." But a few short months after this accolade, the news broke that the ad was a phony—that the Volvo in the row of cars had been artificially reinforced to ensure that it would "win" the contest.

The car-crushing contest had been portrayed as a real event, but some Austin residents paid by Volvo's ad agency to be members of the crowd of spectators had their doubts right from the start. At the time of the filming in June 1990, they contacted the Texas Attorney General's Office to report that something was not quite right.

After an investigation, Attorney General Jim Mattox charged that Volvo had fabricated the ads in more ways than one. First, he contended that the car-crushing contest was not an actual exhibition, but rather a dramatization—which should have been clearly disclosed in the ad. He also accused Volvo of reinforcing its station wagon with lumber or steel to withstand *Bear Foot*'s pounding. Moreover, he said that the structural pillars in the competing vehicles had been intentionally cut or weakened. In court papers, Mattox charged that "the car-crushing competition was a hoax and a sham."

Volvo's Immediate Response.   Appearing before the press in Austin, Attorney General Mattox was joined by William Hoover, senior vice president, Volvo Cars of North America. Hoover admitted that because the Austin event was staged for the purpose of filming, modifications had been made to the vehicles to make sure the production crew's safety was not compromised and to allow the Volvo to withstand the repeated runs by the "monster truck" required for filming. He went on to state that Volvo had built its reputation on honesty and candor and that the company never intended to produce a deceptive or misleading ad. Hoover ended his remarks by thanking the attorney general for bringing the matter to Volvo's attention so that appropriate action could be taken.

"It was unfortunate that we did not label this advertisement as a dramatization," said Hoover. "It would be even more unfortunate, however, if our agreement to withdraw the advertisement at this time created any doubt about the real-world safety of Volvo cars." The provisions of the company's agreement with the state of Texas included the voluntary withdrawal of the ad, reimbursement to the Attorney General's Office for its investigative costs and legal fees, and the publication of a corrective statement.

Volvo purchased space in 19 Texas daily newspapers, *The Wall Street Journal,* and *USA Today* to explain its decision to withdraw the ad. The disclaimer was in the form of an open letter from Joseph L. Nicolato, president and chief executive of Volvo Cars of North America. "We are proud of the strength of our Volvos, but even they cannot withstand being run over so many times by a 'monster truck,' " wrote Nicolato.

Internal Review. Volvo North America, at the instigation of Pehr Gyllenhammer, chairman of the Swedish parent company, initiated an internal review of the performance of its own officials, as well as the conduct of Scali McCabe Sloves, its New York-based ad agency for over two decades; the production company hired by Scali; and of others connected with the production of the ad. As the organization ultimately in charge of the ad, Scali accepted responsibility and shortly thereafter resigned the Volvo account.

Scali's Chairman Martin Sloves stated: "My partners and I, and many others in our firm, have over the last 23 years dedicated countless hours working with Volvo to establish it as one of the most respected and admired brand names in North America. Because of this long working relationship, it is of great personal and professional concern that our actions in no way diminish the value and reputation of the Volvo name. To this end, it is imperative that we resign and accept ultimate responsibility for what happened. Now is not the time to point fingers at anyone. We have established that the issue is only the making of this advertisement—and in no way a reflection on the strength, durability, and safety of the Volvo automobile, on the integrity of the Volvo corporation, or on any previous advertising done by this agency."

Aftermath. Volvo chose a new advertising agency, New York-based Messner Vetere Berger Carey Schmetterer, to handle its $40 million account. Company officials and outside image experts see little damage so far to Volvo's image—although the transition to a new ad agency after so many years may be tricky.

For example, Larry Ackerman, a partner in the identity consultant firm of Anspach Grossman Portugal, does not expect Volvo to suffer much public opinion damage. "I think this whole affair caused more damage to the ad agency—and the image of the advertising world in general—than to Volvo. This incident has set the credibility of the advertising business back 10 years in the mind of the public. But Volvo has built up over the years a solid image as a safe, quality car, and I don't think many will begin to question that just because one of its vehicles may or may not have survived a pounding by a monster truck. I think its image has served it well."

Some Wall Street watchers, however, have expressed concern over the incident. A typical view comes from John Casesa, an analyst for the auto industry at Wertheim Schroder & Co., who keeps a sharp eye on the numbers. He is a bit less sanguine because of the timing of the misleading ad. "Volvo—like Saab and Mercedes—is fighting a tough battle to keep market share now that the Japanese have entered the luxury, or higher-end, car market," he observes. "It's critical that Volvo maintain its image as a very safe car. That image is what makes Volvo stand out; it can't beat the Japanese on quality, price, or performance. If the consumer starts to question that image, it would be dire for sales."

U.S. sales are in decline for virtually all the manufacturers, so to link Volvo's loss of sales entirely to the ad flap may not be fair. The company reports that first-quarter 1991 Volvo sales were down 18.1 percent in the United States; total industry sales were off 16.8 percent. For the same period, total import sales were off 20.4 percent.

Case Example

Burroughs Wellcome: Combating an Accusation

Ever since U.K.-owned Burroughs Wellcome Co. (BW) launched the first and only drug approved by the U.S. Food and Drug Administration (FDA) for use against the lethal AIDS virus, the company has been on a public relations hot seat. Its major problem has been the price of its drug, which has infuriated some in the AIDS-ravaged gay community and, at the least, raised eyebrows among U.S. health officials and members of Congress. Because this is a life-or-death issue, whose constituencies comprise ill people and their families and supporters— who are increasingly organized and vocal—BW may, in fact, have walked into a no-win situation. However, some critics believe the company could have taken steps to reduce its vulnerability to negative publicity.

Not-for-Profit Manufacturer.   To say that Wellcome was poorly prepared to be the object of sustained wrath is putting it mildly: As one of the world's oldest and most respected drug companies, many of Wellcome's research efforts have been devoted to drugs for diseases that are poorly or inadequately treated, including "orphan" drugs. These are drugs for diseases, such as malaria and toxoplasmosis, whose profitability is so marginal that larger pharmaceutical companies do not want to bother developing them.

Burroughs Wellcome Co. is the U.S. subsidiary of the Wellcome Foundation Ltd., founded in the United Kingdom in 1880 by two pharmacists, Silas Burroughs and Henry Wellcome. Part of the legacy left by Sir Henry Wellcome is that profits from the company and its subsidiaries were to be used for medical research, libraries, museums, and other activities related to medicine on a worldwide scale. This led to the creation of the Wellcome Trust, into which 75 percent of all corporate profits are paid for the support of scientific education and medical research. In 1989 alone, $55 million in dividends were distributed to the trust—making it the largest private charitable organization in the United Kingdom. Wellcome has received awards for its commitment to developing orphan drugs as well as four Nobel prizes for medicine for its scientists' outstanding contributions.

In addition to contributions made by the Wellcome Trust, the Burroughs Wellcome Fund, a nonprofit private foundation organized in 1955 in the United States, has provided more than $38.3 million for the advancement of medical knowledge in the country.

A Breakthrough Drug. BW's long experience in researching antivirals (putting it virtually alone among the leading pharmaceutical firms) enabled it to be in a unique position to undertake the investigation for a treatment for AIDS. During the decade before it became apparent that human immunodeficiency virus (HIV) posed a serious public health threat, the company had been developing Zovirax brand acyclovir, an antiviral drug for herpes virus infections. This background, combined with knowledge acquired in the creation of two earlier antiviral agents, provided a strong foundation for BW's AIDS research.

Work began in 1984, soon after the medical community learned what caused the disease. Just three years later, the FDA cleared BW's Retrovir brand zidovudine (AZT) as a treatment for AIDS. In the United Kingdom, the Wellcome Foundation received the prestigious Queen's Award for developing a process for producing the drug in marketable quantities in a short period of time. But in the United States, BW's public relations troubles were just beginning.

Controversy over Pricing.   Based on the price BW initially set for AZT, a year's treatment cost between $8200 and $10,000. The company's justification for this high cost was that it had to recoup the huge expenditures it had made in R&D as well as continue to fund ongoing research. BW had indeed responded to the pressing needs of patients by undertaking a crash program to boost production as quickly as possible.

Under normal circumstances, BW would have spent seven to 10 years devising and perfecting the methods required to make commercial quantities of the drug. It had produced only a fraction of an ounce for its initial demonstration of antiviral activity in the lab, but now tons were needed to supply many thousands of patients. By devoting most of its chemical development resources to Retrovir, BW compressed the time schedule to three years.

In any case, the price of Retrovir unleashed a storm of controversy. According to company spokesperson Kathy Bartlett, "The public didn't understand what was involved with the R&D costs of the new pharmaceutical. We brought the drug to AIDS patients in record time;

its future was uncertain in that no one knew how well it would work; and we didn't have the most efficient manufacturing process in place. Any medication, like AZT, that is taken in daily doses is expensive." The company did implement a patient-assistance program that provided Retrovir at no cost to people who could not afford it and had no insurance. However, the firm did little to publicize this program because other third-party, state, and federal programs were not yet in place and the company knew it was unable to bear the entire burden.

The company underestimated the power of gay activist groups, whose anger was first directed at the U.S. government and drug companies in general for alleged foot-dragging in finding a cure or even treatments. As soon as AZT appeared, the activists seized on BW, labeling it greedy and callous to charge such a high price for the only effective AIDS medication available. After the drug's approval by the FDA, furious anti-Burroughs demonstrations erupted on Wall Street, and Congress called BW executives to Capitol Hill to answer charges of price gouging.

"We hadn't worked with such a well-organized patient community before," says Bartlett of the difficult situation the company faced in 1987. Some media pointed out that BW lacked adequate public relations or lobbying representation in Washington, which it could have used at the time.

Part of the company's problems resulted from making most of the important decisions regarding Retrovir in the United Kingdom. Sir Alfred Shepperd, recently retired chairman of London-based Wellcome PLC, the U.K. operating subsidiary of the Wellcome Trust, designated Retrovir as a special "chairman's project." Hence, the London board made the key decisions about the drug's production and marketing, which proved inappropriate in the important U.S. market. Clearly, this was an instance in which the adage "Think global but act local" should have been followed.

According to Bartlett, "The only country where we had enormous controversy over the price of AZT was the United States. Many other countries in which we market the drug have government-supported medical systems, so the pricing was not a consumer issue."

An Improved Situation. Over time and with experience, BW has been able to take steps to defuse the explosive situation and, to some extent, overcome the negative image that plagued the firm earlier. These include the following:

- *Lower prices.* BW was able to reduce the price of Retrovir by almost 80 percent, to approximately $2200 a year. It accomplished this because of an anticipated growth in the patient population coupled with continued production economies. Moreover, the FDA's approval of a lower dose of AZT has further reduced annual costs for many patients.
- *Washington representation.* BW has hired a former deputy assistant secretary at the U.S. Department of Health and Human Services (of which the FDA is a branch) to look out for BW's interests on Capitol Hill.

- *Proactive stance with the gay community.* BW has complemented its existing educational efforts with an outreach initiative (begun in April 1990) to AIDS groups in the hardest-hit 25 U.S. cities. The range of educational and service programs varies according to the needs of local communities. These may include local information campaigns about the disease; sponsoring "town hall" meetings with AIDS experts; or funding staff positions, such as AIDS counselors or outreach workers. This outreach initiative has broadened the company's existing educational efforts, which focused on services to people with AIDS. The new programs aim to help people in less severe stages of HIV infection or those at risk of becoming infected. Since 1987, BW has provided more than $4.7 million to community-based groups providing service to people with AIDS and for support of educational programs for health-care professionals.

- *Public service ads (PSA).* BW is participating in a public information advertising campaign cosponsored by national medical associations and AIDS service organizations. The campaign consists of radio, print, and outdoor ads that encourage people at risk to learn more about what they can do to manage the infection and maintain a good quality of life (see Figure 9-1).

The ads also direct people to a toll-free national AIDS hot line number, which provides information and referrals to local service providers. The content of the ad campaign was developed after interviews with patients, at-risk people, and primary-care physicians. One militant group, the AIDS Coalition to Unleash Power (ACT-UP), has criticized the PSA campaign on the ground that BW is using it to promote AZT, although the drug is not mentioned in the ads. (ACT-UP also led the protests against the pricing of AZT.) However, most gay publications, including *Outweek*, a high-visibility national magazine, have agreed to run the ads, because they believe the message is both important and accurate.

Case Example

Warner-Lambert: Building Good Will in Africa

As the preceding case suggests, the public has mixed feelings about the pharmaceutical industry. It is seen in two conflicting lights: as a vehicle for alleviating human suffering and, at the same time, as an exploiter of the ill for profit.

While all economic activity is open to criticism, the drug industry has an unusually high public profile because it is dominated by a few large corporations and is extremely profitable. For many years it has attracted attention, favorable and unfavorable, much beyond that which its size might suggest. The conduct of its affairs is without question a matter of public concern and public controversy.

Figure 9-1

The industry's failures (copycat drugs, AIDS treatments, thalidomide, Dalkon Shield) are better remembered than its successes (antibiotics, insulin, Dilantin). An extensive literature, dating mainly from the 1970s and 1980s, shows that medicines with high risks of side effects have been promoted for general use.

In the Third World particularly, European, U.S., and Japanese drug companies have long been accused of dubious marketing practices. Other equally serious charges have been leveled against the industry. Critics allege that medicines not approved by regulatory agencies in the industrialized world have been exported to developing countries. Prices have been called excessive, and transfer pricing has been used to repatriate excessive profits. Most damaging of all, critics contend, Third World countries have been persuaded to spend too much on mainly unnecessary or unsuitable drugs, and too little on vaccines, clean water, and basic sanitation. Watchdog groups want MNC pharmaceutical companies to accept full responsibility for the uses of their prescription drug products in the absence of appropriate local regulations. While the standards of the international pharmaceutical companies in general are higher than those of local firms, the effect on the reputation of the industry as a whole has been markedly negative.

This case example shows how another global pharmaceutical company, Warner-Lambert (W-L), has simultaneously enhanced its own image and that of its industry, while upgrading health education in the Third World.

Finding a New Path: Tropicare.   Coping with the negative perceptions of their industry is a key preoccupation for all multinational drug companies. For a global competitor such as Warner-Lambert, management was forced to confront these issues in the early 1980s, when it decided to open a new plant in Africa. It recognized the image problems associated with its industry in the Third World and adjusted its strategy accordingly. This case study discusses W-L's creation of an unusual health-care program, Tropicare, which was based on four principles: emphasis on preventive self-help, local management participation, a totally noncommercial content, and conformance to international standards.

Tropicare enabled the company to obtain a variety of benefits for itself and for the African countries in which it does business: W-L gained a foothold in new African markets, muted criticism of the pharmaceutical industry's practices in the Third World, won the support of leading multilateral health organizations, and enhanced its own corporate image. At the same time, it has helped raise public health standards in several African nations.

Although W-L's program dealt with health care, its approach can be readily adapted by companies in other industries and in other regions (see box p. 135).

Lessons from Warner-Lambert's Image Building

Companies interested in creating a grass-roots program (in such areas as health care, pollution control, or agricultural development) should consider these guidelines from the W-L executives responsible for the development of Tropicare:

- *Use a planned, rather than ad hoc, approach.* Base activities in each country on carefully constructed strategic plans designed to achieve specific objectives.

- *Coordinate the program closely with overall corporate goals.* In W-L's case, the public relations benefits from Tropicare help to increase shareholder value, sales, profits, market share, and productivity. They also enhance the company's reputation and build employee loyalty. Tropicare also helps fulfill W-L's corporate creed: "to achieve leadership in advancing the health and well-being of people throughout the world."

- *Make the program proactive rather than reactive.* W-L took the initiative—in many cases, plowing new ground—to make Tropicare part of several countries' health education systems.

- *Strive for quantifiable results.* W-L has strengthened its bottom line, thanks to Tropicare, by virtue of gaining easier entry into countries that might have been less hospitable otherwise.

- *Seek the participation of outsiders who can add to the program's stature.* W-L worked with many international health organizations and local village groups to build and support the Tropicare program in Africa.

- *Enlist top management in the effort.* Without the active involvement of the CEO and other senior executives, any image-building program, but especially one overseas, will almost certainly fail.

- *Take steps to ensure your ethics are beyond reproach.* W-L management realized from the start that industry critics—not to mention the host governments themselves—could have assailed Tropicare for being a duplicitous marketing scheme. To combat this skepticism, W-L devised and did not deviate from a strict standard of ethical guidelines where the program was concerned. The company also worked on building trust by working in a partnership capacity with various constituencies—from the UN to the host governments to the local residents.

Background and Organization.   Tropicare came into being as part
of W-L's overall strategy for Africa. When the company decided to
expand its business in Africa beyond the English-speaking countries of
Kenya and Nigeria, it realized that it would have to do more than simply
sell products to achieve lasting success. As the first U.S. pharmaceutical
manufacturer in West Africa—when it opened a $5.4 million plant in
Dakar, Senegal—W-L knew it had a "unique presence" in the region.
"Such a presence creates very special responsibilities for us in helping to
meet basic health-care needs," said Chairman and CEO Joseph Williams
at the plant dedication.

W-L committed itself to concentrate on basic drugs at its Dakar
facility. The plant began making antimalarials for the African market in
mid-1983, complementing the plans of the region's governments to
make the treatment of malaria one of their top health priorities.
Subsequently, the company began producing anti-asthmatics, anti-
infectives, analgesics, and cough and cold medications. Many of these
preparations are among those the World Health Organization (WHO)
has recommended for local manufacture.

Tropicare was and is a completely noncommercial program to provide
training and education for local health-care providers and community
leaders. It consists of a series of slides and audiocassettes that provide a
very clear, simple, repetitive message stressing preventive techniques
and demonstrating a range of treatments for prevailing diseases,
including both drug and nondrug therapies. The subjects include
management of malaria, fever control, water-borne diseases, and
accidents to children in the home.

To ensure the quality and the nonpromotional character of the
audiovisuals, W-L organized in each major country a Joint Therapeutic
Commission (JTC) that included experts from academia and national
and international health organizations. Formally launched in Senegal,
Tropicare subsequently was instituted in the Ivory Coast, Zaire,
Cameroon, Nigeria, and Kenya. The initial commitment was for three
years, although it continued beyond that period. (It is currently winding
down in Africa, but is being implemented elsewhere.) Over the first four
years, 17 audiovisual programs were produced.

The JTCs decided on the topics and oversaw the production and
dissemination of the programs. Drafts of the scripts and the
corresponding slides were provided by W-L to the JTCs, which gave their
approval for distribution. This local control over the content was
essential, in W-L's view, because only local government officials and
medical experts know the actual conditions in a particular country. By
involving such people deeply in the development of the training
materials, W-L avoids the common pitfall of "taking over." This keeps the
Tropicare program from being considered just another well-meaning,
but ineffective, instrument of foreign aid, one that is politely accepted
but not used.

W-L's main role was simply to facilitate the use of African expertise.
Thus, in each country, in addition to the programs produced locally, the

JTC approved some programs produced in other countries. W-L assumed all costs of development and dissemination to health workers in the field by its own network of representatives. Each medical representative devoted one day a week to Tropicare.

Management took strong steps to ensure that the medical representatives observed the noncommercial nature of the Tropicare program. For instance, all W-L employees were required to sign an Ethical Charter acknowledging their awareness of the ban on sales promotion.

Assessing Benefits and Costs. The first evaluation was done in mid-1987 and indicated that Tropicare had exceeded expectations.

The chief benefit for the host countries is that an estimated 200,000 health-care workers and other interested people viewed at least one of the 17 programs. And a large but undetermined number saw or heard more than one, and perhaps many, of the programs. (This figure was based on W-L's own observations as well as on estimates provided by local and international health organizations operating in the field.)

Tropicare's ripple effects have been widespread. Some of the programs are also being used by other international health organizations operating on the continent. Among these are the Belgian government development agency, the U.S. AID and Center for Disease Control, the International Children's Center (Paris), the Churches of Christ (U.S.), the schools of medicine and public health of the universities of Paris and Bordeaux, the Senegal and Haiti Catholic relief organizations, Tanzania Christian Medical Center, and the French National Institute for Scientific Medical Research.

These results square well with the program's goal of training people in the community to use existing resources to help keep disease at bay. This is critical, says Aracelia Vila, Tropicare's project director, because "in most African nations, a shortage of trained medical personnel is the weak link in primary care."

For W-L, there were both substantial costs and benefits. During the first four years, the firm invested around $1 million to cover production of the audio-visual materials, travel, and the time devoted to the program by company representatives. On the benefit side, however, were the following achievements:

- *Relationships with opinion leaders.* Through the JTCs, W-L developed excellent relationships with the most important opinion leaders in each country. The JTCs consisted of a mix of top government policymakers; independent medical experts, such as deans of the local teaching hospitals and pharmacy schools; representatives of the nursing and midwife professions; community health workers; and physicians responsible for health care in rural areas.

- *Relationships with international and nongovernmental groups.* Tropicare won a positive reception at the WHO and was formally identified as "an industry contribution" in the 1984 official progress report on the WHO's Action Program on Essential Drugs. Local representatives of the WHO, the United Nations Children's Fund (UNICEF), and the U.S. Agency for International Development (AID) also participated in JTC activities.

- *Recognition by U.S. government.* Tropicare was awarded an $80,000 grant by the U.S. Overseas Private Investment Corp. (OPIC). W-L used this grant to produce an audiovisual program, *A Guide to Good Pharmaceutical Practice in Africa,* directed at health-care and government officials, as well as a complementary program called *Health for All,* the only such program addressed to the general public in Africa.

  The OPIC/Tropicare programs were seen on television in some countries, reaching audiences in urban areas. *Health for All* was also shown in the waiting rooms of dispensaries and clinics and at community functions.

- *Better understanding of the market.* W-L's own personnel became more aware that the potential of a market is directly linked to improving local health conditions and standards.

Solving Problems. Over the course of the years the program was under way, Tropicare's creators faced a variety of issues, which had to be solved as they arose. For example, at the beginning, when W-L proposed to set up the JTCs, several key health leaders asked for free or noncommercially priced drugs, as they considered obtaining drugs for their countries a very high priority. It was sometimes difficult for W-L to explain to these officials that this was neither the intent of the Tropicare project nor a realistic possibility. However, through dialogue, W-L succeeded in forging a consensus that the Tropicare initiative, without entailing the supplying of drugs, could be of mutual benefit and could lead to a long-term improvement in public health.

W-L also encountered difficulties in finalizing some programs because of changes in the local political situation. Several JTCs replaced their members several times within a few years as a consequence of shifts in the political power structure. In the worst cases, programs were delayed or never finalized.

It was sometimes necessary to change the attitude of the viewers, because many expected that before viewing the programs they would be offered a free lunch or cocktail. This expectation grew out of their experience with other presentations by pharmaceutical companies, which were almost always promotional shows. A drug manufacturer offering a truly educational, no-sales-promotion-attached program was something altogether new. Thus, within the health-care community, in dispensaries and hospitals, W-L's commitment was at first viewed with suspicion.

Such difficulties, however, were only temporary, not insurmountable obstacles. Overall, the program went smoothly and was readily accepted for the objective, easy-to-understand information it presented. It also had favorable spillover into W-L's business operations in Africa. As Alain Mathieu, W-L's director for Africa at the time the program was launched, explains: "Tropicare is a unique regional approach to serving the public. If we were not involved this way, it would be harder to identify local priorities, which is what companies do everywhere to help give people what they want."

Tropicare's close alignment to bottom-line thinking about the products most needed in various countries has helped management convince governments that Tropicare is more than just a charity. Indeed, it represents a long-term commitment to improve living standards and create more affluent customers for W-L's products.

The company also stresses the practical link between Tropicare and the productivity of the local W-L work force. "Our employees face health problems themselves," says Mathieu. "They are no less affected by the condition of medical services. If we wish to motivate employees, we must connect their work to improvements in living standards."

He concludes that "our image as a U.S. company in French-speaking Africa has definitely improved. Tropicare is one reason that we are now accepted as business partners in all the communities we serve."

The Future of Tropicare.   Phase I of the Tropicare program concentrated on Africa, with the initial commitment planned to last three to four years. W-L decided in 1988 to complete all programs still in the planning stage and to ensure their continued dissemination, but to move on, in various ways, from the original Tropicare countries. Each W-L representative in these countries is now devoting only one day every two weeks to Tropicare, focusing on new health-care workers, because most of the established workers have already seen the majority of the programs. W-L also provides duplication of the audiovisuals and the regular transportation of audiovisual projectors to different communities.

In addition, W-L undertook to expand the program. Since mid-1988, Tropicare has been implemented in three smaller African countries—Mali, Ghana, and Burkina Faso—reaching an additional 2000 or more health-care workers. No JTCs were established in these countries, but the clearance for dissemination of the audiovisual materials is done by the Ministry of Health. For instance, the Tropicare program *Control of Acute Diarrhea* is now being used by the Ministry of Health of Mali in a preventive campaign. Programs on sexually transmitted diseases and home accidents involving children have also been introduced.

A major expansion of Tropicare, Phase II, was undertaken with the transplantation of the program to Latin America in 1988. The first country in that region to receive the program was Colombia. The Colombian minister of health approved plans for the local JTC's initial project, which consisted of three new audiovisuals on hypertension, malaria, and road accidents. These will be used in a pilot program agreed upon by W-L and the Ministry of Health in the city of Cali and the surrounding region of Valle del Cauca, which offers racial, climatic, and epidemiological characteristics similar to the country as a whole. It is therefore a good launch point, for it allows the company to smooth out any problems before taking Tropicare to other parts of the country.

W-L's objectives for the future include testing Tropicare in a Southeast Asian nation. Beyond this, the company intends to seek partnerships with other governments to carry Tropicare beyond its own reach and to maximize the investment embodied in its existing library of audiovisuals, rather than undertake the preparation of new programs. Understandably, the audiovisuals will be modified for new countries.

W-L believes that the OPIC grant and the establishment of JTCs in Africa and Colombia are examples of the cooperation that can develop between government and the private sector, both at home and abroad, to meet key national health policy objectives. It is confident that the project rests on a solid ground of mutual trust and in the shared desire to demonstrate that such partnerships are possible.

10
Being a Good Corporate Citizen

The concept of good corporate citizenship promises to expand in both meaning (beyond philanthropy) and scope (beyond domestic markets) in the 1990s. Indeed, it is already becoming one of the key attributes of global corporations operating in a global marketplace.

In the United States there has long been an emphasis on private sector support of the arts, education, and other social causes not adequately funded by the government. Even though the rash of mergers and acquisitions in the 1980s has reduced the number of large corporations in the country, the total donated by business to U.S. charities, schools, museums, theaters, and other nonprofit organizations (nonprofits) reached an estimated $5.6 billion in 1989.

But some analysts and corporate leaders predict that corporations aiming to distinguish themselves in this decade, both in the United States and elsewhere, will do more than simply give money: They will move to establish partnerships with nonprofits and civic leaders by encouraging executives to join the boards of local groups and participate in finding solutions to local problems.

Such an approach could not be more timely: Solutions to many of the world's environmental problems—global warming, ozone depletion, and acid rain—clearly will require international cooperation. So will most of the world's other ills: the deadly and astronomically expensive AIDS pandemic, global poverty, and traffic in illegal drugs. Increased privatization and government cutbacks in social services in many countries offer numerous opportunities for companies to make substantive contributions to solving such problems at both the local and world levels. Not incidentally, they can enhance their image in the eyes of employees, customers, and government leaders.

Conservative governments in Europe are welcoming private sector programs to provide job training for inner-city youth, to meet the needs of immigrants, and to solve massive pollution problems. And in Eastern Europe, where the lines between the private and public sectors are just now being drawn, corporations have a unique opportunity to take a leadership role in shaping new societies.

MNCs to Assume Social Responsibility

With consciousness about the environment and other issues expanding around the world, there is a growing expectation that corporations will take on their share of responsibility, according to James Parkel, director of IBM's Office of Corporate Support Programs. As he puts it, "Employees don't want to work for companies that have no social conscience, customers don't want to do business with companies that pollute the environment or are notorious for shoddy products and practices, and communities don't welcome companies that aren't good corporate citizens. Many shareholder issues are socially driven."

Parkel contends that corporations fit into one of three styles of corporate social policy. At the lowest level are firms that acquire a social policy only when faced with a crisis. When there is a product failure, recall, or legal problem, such corporations attempt to mop up the damage with a public relations campaign that trumpets concern for social and community values. When the problem goes away, so do the philosophy and the concern. At the second level are companies with long traditions of philanthropy, integrity, and community standing. Their missions remain fuzzy, however, and their efforts are piecemeal. One year such a firm will support a public school initiative, and the next year, when results are disappointing, it will cut back its support. Most companies fit into this category, Parkel believes.

At the top level, he notes, are corporations such as IBM—and a relatively few others—that have a social vision and a planned long-term social policy. (IBM's program is described in detail on pp. 146–148.)

Social Problems Impede Business Activity

Edmund Burke, director of the Center for Corporate Community Relations at Boston College, says there is growing recognition that many social factors—such as local attitudes toward business, education levels of the available work force, and environmental regulations—can get in the way of conducting business successfully. The reason many U.S. companies have thrown their support behind the improvement of education is that education is a long-term investment in a quality work force, he says. "To achieve your business vision you have to have a social vision." To encourage such vision, the Center for Corporate Community Relations, which has helped many firms improve community relations in the United States, has launched a globalization roundtable at which company representatives exchange ideas and information on their philanthropic and community affairs activities around the world.

Corporations can no longer take a "we don't do that" stance when faced with requests for social, environmental, and educational assistance, according to Dr. Delwyn Roy, president and chief executive officer of the Hitachi Foundation. "The world is changing," says Roy. "Every firm needs a social investment strategy."

Craig Smith, editor and publisher of the Seattle-based *Corporate Philanthropy Report,* says, "In the future, a corporate show of goodwill won't be enough. People will want to see results. The key issue is whether companies are going to 'get by'—throwing a few crumbs to nonprofits—or whether they're going to be forced really to be a benefit to the communities where they're operating."

Community Involvement

The experience of Japanese corporations in the United States illustrates dramatically that corporate philanthropy is only one aspect of being a good corporate citizen in an overseas market. As the Japanese learned in the 1980s, writing generous checks to prestigious art institutions or universities does not automatically confer on a company the status of good corporate citizen. (Indeed, checkbook philanthropy exposed some Japanese corporations to charges of hypocrisy—that they were trying to buy the hearts and minds of U.S. citizens while taking jobs away from the United States and undermining entire industries.)

Being a good corporate citizen also means involving the company actively in the community, hiring and promoting people in a fair and nondiscriminatory manner, stimulating the local economy by purchasing from local firms, engaging in local real estate development, and considering the community's interests when making other business decisions.

Craig Smith is currently developing a series of public forums called "Japan at the American Grassroots" in an attempt to help Japanese companies enter civic leadership networks in the United States. The forums also will widen the circle of nonprofits that have one-on-one relationships with local Japanese managers. Despite the dynamic role Japanese companies are playing in the U.S. economy, true partnerships with nonprofits and community leaders have remained "few and far between," he says. In one effort, to gain local acceptance of a new manufacturing facility in Kentucky, Toyota established a day-care center for employees and required its managers to get involved in the community.

Reasons for Noninvolvement. David Owens, vice president at Dentsu Burson-Marsteller, a public relations firm based in New York that serves the communications needs of Japanese companies operating in the United States, says the Japanese Chamber of Commerce and Industry of New York approached his firm in 1989 about helping its members to "improve their standing in the business community." After considering a speakers' bureau and a few other proposals, the Japanese Chamber of Commerce agreed to produce a handbook called *Joining In.* This manual educates members about the tradition of corporate responsibility and philanthropy in the United States, gives instructions on how to set up employee volunteer programs, and encourages involvement at the management level. Such basic education is necessary because there is no established tradition of corporate philanthropic activism in Japan.

"We don't even have a word for 'philanthropy' as it's understood in the United States," says Peter Kamura, executive secretary of the nonprofit Japan Center for International Exchange, based in Tokyo and New York. "Japanese companies do far more for the benefit of their employees and families than U.S. companies. That has been more or less the corporate practice of philanthropy in Japan."

Joining In suggests another reason Japanese and other foreign companies and individuals do not get involved is that no one asks them. Notes the handbook: "They are too shy and are afraid of making an uninvited approach. One result is that Japan-based corporations and their resident executives in America suffer from the image of being disengaged. 'They don't mingle' and 'They always take, but they never give' are phrases that Americans sometimes use in reference to Japanese in their community who do not participate in community activities."

According to a recent Japan Society/SRI International survey, 89 percent of Americans believe that Japanese companies operating in the United States should be just as involved in their local communities as American companies. However, according to the same survey, half of Japanese companies in the United States—mostly small, new, and service-oriented businesses—describe themselves as inactive corporate citizens. The large consumer-goods corporations tend to be more active, especially if they are located in rural areas.

One third of the larger Japanese companies describes itself as somewhat active corporate citizens, and one in five describes itself as an extremely active or very active corporate citizen.

Case Example

How Two Japanese Firms Handle U.S. Giving

Two of the most active Japanese participants in U.S. philanthropic and community activities are Hitachi America Ltd. and Toyota Motor Manufacturing.

In 1985, after operating for 25 years in the United States, Hitachi Ltd. established the Hitachi Foundation, which has a current endowment of about $25 million. Since then the foundation has awarded over $5 million in grants to support national and local efforts to increase international understanding, foster economic development, improve the quality of education, and increase opportunities for women and minorities. The foundation has supported a school program that teaches students about world geography with playground maps, funded economic development projects for low-income women and minority women through the Ms. Foundation, and provided assistance to an organization that helps neighborhood businesses find markets for their services.

The firm's headquarters in Tarrytown, New York, and various Hitachi divisions and subsidiaries across the United States also have Employee Community Action Committees, which channel small grants ($500–$5000) to community organizations. For example, the Tarrytown committee has given money for clothing and a basketball court for young, emotionally disturbed boys living in a local group home. It also has provided volunteers to help with career counseling.

The annual budget for all Employee Community Action Committees is $100,000. The Hitachi Foundation also provides matching funds for the local committees.

The focus of Toyota Foundation spending is narrower. In 1990, the Toyota Foundation awarded $650,000 in grants, mostly to support math and science programs for exceptional high school students. The parent company in Japan has provided financial support for artistic and cultural events at Lincoln Center and the Metropolitan Museum of Art. Akikazu Kida, group manager of external affairs for Toyota Motor Corporate Services in New York, says the parent company has also donated $2 million recently to the National Center for Family Literacy for a program that allows high school dropouts to get their diplomas while their children attend preschool.

When Toyota chose Georgetown, Kentucky, as the site for a $1.1 billion manufacturing facility in 1985, CEO Fujio Cho had to act quickly to win acceptance in the face of negative publicity. Many local and state residents were irate over the incentive package that had been offered to the company, at a time when the state faced serious economic problems.

Toyota sought to build trust in its new community in a variety of ways, including the following:

- Forming a high-level liaison committee to meet with the mayor, city council, and other officials on a regular basis
- Making community involvement a requirement for its managers
- Hiring locally and retaining Kentucky State University to manage screening of potential employees
- Voluntarily adopting the stringent affirmative-action policies of federal government contractors and encouraging suppliers to do the same
- Establishing a day-care center for employees' children
- Agreeing to pay $10.2 million to Scott County public schools over the next 20 years in lieu of property taxes (the company's property was not taxable under the incentive plan) and awarding $1 million to residents to build a new community center
- Founding a "Model Supplier Program" to help suppliers in Kentucky and other states establish and maintain quality standards
- Having staff regularly meet with local water managers and environmental groups to discuss the company's use of resources and environmental problems.

Some Japanese firms still find that their gestures of good corporate citizenship meet with misunderstanding or disapproval. For example, Japanese banks in San Francisco were criticized after giving millions of dollars for earthquake relief because they turned down a number of lower-profile requests by local groups. Nevertheless, the Japan Society/SRI International survey indicates that corporate philanthropy and community involvement do improve a company's image. Some 87 percent of the companies surveyed that described themselves as extremely or very active as corporate citizens said they were viewed positively by their communities. In contrast, only 31 percent of the inactive companies felt they were so regarded.

Case Example

IBM's Approach to Corporate Philanthropy

IBM has a long history of community service that can be traced back to founder Thomas Watson. One of the world's top corporate givers ($148 million in 1990), IBM's best-known philanthropic efforts are its donations of computer equipment worth millions of dollars to U.S. schools and its encouragement of employee volunteerism. About half of

IBM's U.S. work force are volunteers, and the company offers a limited number of paid leaves to professionals and managers interested in doing extended community service.

In 1988, IBM undertook a major two-year reevaluation of its corporate-responsibility activities. The company consulted outside experts, commissioned surveys, asked those who ran local IBM programs around the world to rank their priorities, and finally brought together managers and professionals from offices in 10 countries for a meeting. The goal was to make IBM's social agenda more forceful and effective.

"We believe the strategic planning and measurement disciplines we use to run the business can be adapted to corporate social responsibility with good effect," said James Parkel in a speech at the Keystone Conference in Colorado in October 1990, which addressed the issue of building a generation of MBAs skilled in solving social problems.

IBM named Parkel, a 28-year IBM veteran who most recently served as employee relations director, to head up its Office of Corporate Support, restructured the process for setting annual philanthropy budgets and grantmaking decisions, and committed itself to a "strategic" focus on two major issues worldwide—education and the environment. IBM has already worked in these areas, but plans to focus its efforts even more in the future for greater impact.

The company's track record in education hardly needs introduction. Many university computer science departments trace their origins to IBM grants, while sponsored research and grants helped move many academic departments of chemistry, physics, and math into the information age. IBM's 1990 spending for high schools and elementary schools last year in the United States included $170,000 in hardware and software to improve educational quality in Georgia schools and $20 million (spaced over several years) in software, hardware, and support for teacher education and curriculum development in California.

In several Asian countries, IBM has helped university scholars gain access to sophisticated data bases, and donated computers to help university managers improve productivity. The computer company gives fellowships to Asian students who want to do graduate study in Japan (one new program focuses on natural sciences and engineering). IBM is also helping to bring Eastern European university scientists into the information age.

On the environmental front, IBM's activities serve two broad purposes: helping to solve environmental problems by applying computer technology to them and, by participating in the solution to problems, finding out what resources scientists need to make further progress. One major project is a European effort to clear the polluted River Elbe; an IBM professional is "on loan" to the project for five years. Similar programs are being implemented in Brazil and in the Third World. In the United States, IBM made a major five-year commitment to the Atlanta Botanical Gardens, funded environmental education at the Georgia Nature Conservancy, and provided 1600 volunteers to clean up the Kansas City Zoo.

Education and the environment are the two global themes IBM is concerned with as a corporation, but the firm's regional and local offices exercise their own judgment about what to fund. The contributions committees in each country and the manager of community relations at each plant may designate a local environmental or educational project. They do not, however, have to focus on these two themes if there is some other pressing issue in their community they wish to fund, say, in the arts, public health, or job retraining.

In the United States, Europe, Africa, and the Middle East, scientists, engineers, managers, and other professionals may apply for paid leave to do volunteer service, as the person working on the River Elbe project is doing. IBM employees in Japan can take up to 12 days off each year to perform social service.

Parkel says the company is trying to better integrate its donations of cash, equipment, and personnel while making a greater effort to ensure that the community also "brings something to the table." If IBM were to build a recreation center in a tough, inner-city section of Philadelphia as an outright gift, he says, it would be a casualty of neglect and vandalism in two weeks. If, however, IBM helps build the center in partnership with members of the community, the project has much brighter prospects for long-term success.

IBM matches employee gifts up to $5000 on a two-to-one basis and donates computer systems to nonprofit organizations at which company employees volunteer through the Fund for Community Service. Last year in the United States, IBM made cash and equipment contributions worth $4.8 million under this program, which is being implemented in other parts of the world as well.

Case Example

H.B. Fuller: International Philanthropy on a Small Scale

H.B. Fuller, a worldwide manufacturer of adhesives, sealants, and coatings, with 1990 sales of $792 million, has a considerably smaller corporate giving program than IBM, but it too is considered a leader in good corporate citizenship. Its total corporate giving and community affairs budget totaled $642,000 in 1990; in the United States, 5 percent of the previous year's pretax earnings are distributed by the company's foundation and locally at each plant; outside the United States, the community affairs budget is set regionally in Europe and Latin America, based on profitability.

"We believe our philosophy of community involvement applies not only to the part of the company operating in the United States, but also to our worldwide business," says Karen Muller, director of community affairs for H.B. Fuller. Muller adds that the company's commitment to community affairs is "internally driven," not motivated by external expectations.

The company has a U.S. foundation, the H.B. Fuller Co. Foundation, which decides how to distribute most of the money. A lesser amount is allocated to local community affairs councils to distribute to community projects. Internationally, a fixed percentage of pretax earnings is spent in overseas markets by the firm's local community affairs councils. Muller says H.B. Fuller is discussing the possibility of making the foundation international in scope. By centrally distributing 5 percent of worldwide pretax profits, the company would be able "to allocate resources based on need rather than [local] profitability."

H.B. Fuller's community involvement takes place at the grass-roots level. The community affairs councils are composed almost exclusively of rank-and-file employees. Plant managers generally do not participate in the community affairs councils, allowing employees to run this outreach program instead.

Outside the United States, there often "is no organization you can hand a check to," says Muller. "Offering skills can be more important than money." Therefore, employees may oversee charitable projects themselves, which stimulates their initiative, creativity, independence, and social consciousness, as well as helping the community. One result is improved morale and greater pride in their employer.

These benefits are common. In a study of 188 companies, a Columbia University School of Business professor, David Lewin, concluded that productivity and employee morale were significantly higher in corporations that were very involved in their communities.

Susan Thomas, communications manager at the Center for Corporate Community Relations at Boston College, says local employees are a great resource for companies. They understand and are familiar with the needs and issues in the community. In fact, she says, one mistake companies often make is not to allow enough local autonomy in corporate citizenship matters.

H.B. Fuller's Muller notes that the concept of community affairs remains foreign to many employees in Europe, particularly where companies have not been called on in the past to take an active part in local affairs. According to Muller, when the company set up community affairs councils at its European plants, some local work councils, which represent employee interests, interpreted the call to volunteerism as a form of exploitation, using employees to market the company. The strict separation of business and personal life in countries like France, where family pictures are rarely displayed on desks, also creates difficulties.

Alan Christie, community affairs manager for Levi Strauss & Co. in Brussels, found much the same thing when dealing with European personnel. "Community-involvement teams are more concerned with fund-raising than with the type of volunteer work common in the United States," he says. "People here are more comfortable one stage removed from the issues they are helping to deal with." He attributes this to the nature of the European workplace, which is not considered a "focus for leisure activities." Employees do not see why they should engage in these activities under the aegis of their employer.

The boundaries between the government, the private sector, and the nonprofit sector are just now being drawn in Europe and are not always clear, notes Muller. In Austria, for example, the plant manager convinced the company's Community Affairs Council not to award a grant to an environmental nonprofit organization because it might someday act as a watchdog for the government. In Munich, where H.B. Fuller has a solvent plant near a residential area, the Community Affairs Council was also concerned about avoiding the appearance of trying to wield too much influence through its philanthropic activities.

Case Example

After the Takeover: Philanthropy at Pillsbury

Another issue in an era of mergers and acquisitions is the takeover of a company with a strong commitment to philanthropy. The United Kingdom's Grand Metropolitan PLC learned the hard way about the importance of an acquired company's reputation for corporate giving. In 1988, when it was battling to acquire Minneapolis-based Pillsbury, Grand Met was hurt by comparisons with Pillsbury, which was known as a generous local donor. It was assumed that "outsiders" would cut the community programs once they were in charge. Grand Met was also adversely affected by the presence in Minneapolis of a vigorous tradition of progressive politics and the leadership of a business sector known for charitable giving, including such companies as 3M Corp., Dayton Hudson, and Control Data. Dozens of nonprofits in the area rallied to help Pillsbury. Small groups met with its management to ask questions and discuss strategies. Nonprofits wrote letters, which they delivered at a rally at Pillsbury headquarters, to the company and to Minnesota governor Rudy Perpich. They also instituted a media blitz and sent letters to the editors of all the state newspapers.

In the end, Grand Met took what was apparently an unprecedented action: It agreed in writing to maintain Pillsbury's charitable programs at current levels. But the focus of Pillsbury's giving has changed in the three years since the merger. It now includes, in both the United States and the United Kingdom, disadvantaged youth—Grand Met's traditional preference, as well as world hunger—long Pillsbury's main area of emphasis.

In the United States, Grand Met inherited the extensive community-relations programs of Pillsbury's various subsidiaries, which not only make direct donations but also provide product and advertising support. Total outlays average about $10 million annually. Historically, these programs had close ties to the local communities where the subsidiaries are active both as employers and as customers for supply operations. Thus, Pillsbury itself works to combat hunger; Alpo's programs concentrate on animal welfare; Pearle Vision Center assists the vision impaired; Heublein is concerned mainly with alcoholism; Haagen-Daz contributes to various youth programs; and Burger King tries to improve education. Over time, a clear focus for Grand Met's U.S. companies has emerged—that of assisting disadvantaged people, with particular emphasis on children.

Three types of activities comprise the company's community services in the United States—corporate philanthropy, employee volunteerism, and community outreach. Corporate philanthropy consists of charitable giving and corporate monetary and product donations. Employee (and retiree) volunteerism often takes place in conjunction with corporate contributions of money or products, consistent with the company's charitable giving "focus areas." As a result, Grand Met's U.S. acquisitions are continuing to pursue community interests related to their chief lines of business, within overall guidelines set by the parent company's emphasis on disadvantaged constituencies. Community outreach is reflected in sponsorship of a wide range of activities, from the local Special Olympics to a candlelight vigil to highlight children's issues, and from guide dogs for the visually impaired to rescue missions for disasters occurring in the United States and elsewhere.

How Much to Give

In the United States, companies donate an average of 1.67 percent of their pretax earnings to charitable organizations, but some give 5 percent or more, according to Maureen McGowan of the Washington-based Council on Foundations. The Dayton Hudson department store chain, for example, gives 5 percent, and ice cream maker Ben and Jerry's gives 7 percent. In the Minneapolis area, many companies belong to the "Two Percent Club" and the "Five Percent Club," depending on their level of corporate donations.

In an ideal world, U.S. companies would contribute an equal amount overseas, but their giving levels internationally are far lower. In Europe, where H.B. Fuller only recently introduced community affairs councils, no percentage levels have been set for donations, Muller says. In Latin America, about 2.5 percent of pretax earnings are earmarked for community affairs. H.B. Fuller had planned to raise spending to 5 percent there, but Muller notes that the company's giving program has been hindered by the lack of an infrastructure to receive and manage donations and by lack of understanding from employees. Workers sometimes want to know why the company is giving away money instead of raising wages or why it is undertaking a community project instead of paying for the medical care of an employee's child. The company tries to explain that all employees will benefit from improving the whole community.

Some observers believe that the Japanese, newly converted to American-style philanthropy and community relations, may set the pace for increased global spending in the future. The Japanese government is considering allowing deductions for foreign-bound charitable donations. In

1990, the powerful Keidanren business organization formed a "One Percent Club" to encourage Japanese companies to spend 1 percent of their pretax profits on philanthropic activities in the United States and around the world. Burke, of the Center for Corporate Community Relations, says that while 1 percent is below the level of domestic spending by U.S. companies, it is above that of global spending by many firms. Burke believes this Japanese initiative will put pressure on all companies to increase their giving globally.

Hitachi Ltd. recently gave $1.5 million to the European Parliament for capital improvements to buildings and to expand the Parliament's research capabilities. Delwyn Roy of the Hitachi Foundation says there is "a lot of momentum building" to make the U.S. foundation North American in scope. Including Canada and Mexico in the grant-making would better reflect the "movement of product and people" on the continent in the wake of new trade agreements, he says.

From $85 million in 1987, corporate contributions by Japanese corporations in the United States more than tripled to an estimated $300 million in 1990. Although this reflects an impressive increase, the figure is still less than 6 percent of the $5.6 billion total given by U.S. corporations in their home market.

"Collectively, the Japanese are not much of a force" yet in U.S. corporate philanthropy, says Roy. Nevertheless, he is "cautiously optimistic" that the Japanese share will grow to about one fifth of total U.S. corporate giving in the future.

Top Worldwide Givers by Industry—1989	
Petroleum and gas	$195,718,000
Computers	$194,365,000
Transportation	$172,376,000
Pharmaceuticals	$160,016,000
Chemicals	$149,677,000
Telecommunications	$133,477,000
Banking	$114,770,000
Food and beverages	$113,156,000

SOURCE: The Conference Board.

Promotion and Advertising

Japanese companies probably should avoid cause-related marketing activities (such as tying a product promotion to a charitable cause) because of the sensitivity of Americans to the Japanese economic presence, says Roy. Although he is not against advertising or promotion of philanthropy programs, he does not think they are effective in generating sales. A family will not buy a particular TV or car just because the manufacturer sponsors an event in which their child participates, he contends.

In Roy's view, the best approach to image building is to make a firm commitment to a philanthropic program and let the company's accomplishments speak for themselves. "Let recognition accrue to the project you have aligned yourself with and allow your image to be built on the results," he says.

Sophie Sa, director of the Panasonic (formerly Matsushita) Foundation, adds that in a time of deteriorating trade relations between the United States and Japan, givers should be aware of a U.S. attitude that accuses the Japanese of buying favor. "Japanese companies in the United States will have to use their money carefully and make sure it's philanthropy—and not marketing," she says.

However, Toyota does not agree. In an image-building campaign, Toyota Motor Corporate Services has been running a series of print ads called "Toyota: Investing in the Individual," which highlight a high school basketball team and other individuals who have benefited from Toyota's philanthropic initiatives.

Akikazu Kida, group manager of external affairs for Toyota, says the company decided a campaign about its philanthropic program was the best way to tell Americans about the company behind the product. Toyota deliberately stayed away from highlighting its largest donations, wishing to avoid giving an overbearing impression or inviting criticism that, no matter how much it was spending, it was still not enough. Kida says the examples featured were selected carefully. Instead of focusing on dollars, the advertising depicts the small ways Toyota is helping Americans. As of December 1990, the company had received 5000 requests for information in response to the ads, reports Kida.

Mary Gross, manager of corporate communications at Levi Strauss & Co., says the jeans company will probably be more proactive this year and in the future in promoting its philanthropic programs, which focus on economic development and AIDS. "We don't make it a secret that the end goal of our community involvement is to be a profitable company," she says.

The company's effort will probably take the form of a public relations campaign rather than an advertising campaign, Gross says. It will be aimed at the communities where Levi Strauss does not have facilities, because in those cities where the company has operations people are already aware of its contributions.

The Corporate Foundation: Yes or No?

Should a company establish a foundation as a flagship for its charitable contributions program? The decision depends on each company's particular situation and requires careful analysis.

Foundations not only signal a long-term commitment but also provide stability for giving programs because they are shielded fully or partially from the business cycle. As Hayden Smith of the Council for Aid to Education says in a report entitled "To Have or Have Not . . . A Corporate Foundation," the most compelling reason for creating a foundation is to stabilize the level of charitable giving from year to year. This is done by accumulating a pool of funds not subject (or only partially subject) to the company's annual profits as a corporate budget for charitable giving.

Foundations may also be more efficient in distributing funds than the parent company, which must make charitable donations from repatriated profits. Finally, foundations create distance between the company and the beneficiary so the firm does not appear overly self-serving (e.g., when funding research efforts at a university).

The size of the company and that of its charitable contributions budget are not the most important considerations in the decision to create a foundation or not, according to Smith. Although foundations are associated with the likes of Rockefeller, Ford, and Getty, that does not mean small companies should not think about setting up a foundation in some situations.

A foundation can be fully funded, partially funded or serve as a pass-through vehicle, in which case it does not offer much stability, but it does help to project a stronger philanthropic image for the company. Fully funded foundations have assets sufficiently large that investment earnings are equal to the annual contributions budget. Few of the nearly 1000 corporate foundations in the United States are fully funded. In partially funded foundations, assets are appreciable, but investment earnings on the assets are not enough to cover the contributions budget completely.

Annual budgets in pass-through foundations are determined by the corporation and thus depend partially on earnings. Such budgets are set in much the same way that corporations without foundations establish their annual giving budgets. A foundation mainly provides the company with a higher profile.

From a tax perspective, a foundation's main advantage comes when a corporation has appreciated securities or surplus property it wants to use for funding instead of cash. On the other hand, foundations must adhere strictly to rules governing them or face heavy penalties. One rule requires that foundations distribute at least 5 percent of their assets every year.

For global companies that want to increase their worldwide charitable giving, a U.S.-based foundation offers an added advantage: tax deductibility. Although U.S. companies (including U.S. subsidiaries of foreign corporations) can deduct gifts only if the funds are used in the United States, this rule does not apply to foundations. Thus for companies with significant business and profits in the United States, a U.S. foundation can make sound economic and philanthropic sense.

Certainly, for image-building purposes, "having a foundation and doing good deeds through a foundation may be important, even if the foundation is merely a 'pass-through' entity," Smith writes. "It projects a positive image with regard to social responsibility and good citizenship, and promotes the notion that the company is philanthropically minded and that it cares about its communities."

Employee Contributions

Do not overlook employee contributions as a way to boost your donations to international and local organizations. Last year in the United States, workplace campaigns by United Way and other organizations raised more than $2.7 billion for domestic charities.

As the nonprofit sector grows internationally, organizations are being put into place around the world to conduct workplace campaigns for contributions and payroll deductions by employees.

United Way, which runs most workplace campaigns in the United States, now has 32 chapters in 25 countries. Usually once every year, the chapters, representing an umbrella group of local and international nonprofits, will conduct a fund-raising campaign among employees with the consent of the employer. Employers often provide some ratio of matching funds. These funds are then distributed by United Way to the nonprofit organizations.

United Way International also provides technical assistance for budding nonprofit agencies and trains them in fund-raising practices.

Although United Way has a virtual monopoly on U.S. workplace campaigns, alternative fund-raising campaigns, representing a broader range of interests (United Way mainly fund-raises for local social service agencies), are making headway. International Service Agencies (ISA), of Camby, Indiana, conducts workplace campaigns in the United States to benefit international organizations such as Save the Children, Project HOPE, and CARE. The ISA has conducted campaigns for IBM and Apple Computer and participated in workplace campaigns for 24 state governments. The

ISA has also conducted workplace campaigns in the foreign subsidiaries of U.S. companies and is expanding its efforts internationally.

"Corporations and foundations continue to support the ISA member agencies with corporate and foundation grants," says Betty Stratton, director of development at ISA. "However, most charity dollars are contributed by individuals, with a significant portion being contributed through corporate-sanctioned employee giving. Last year, workplace campaigns for domestic charities raised more than $2.7 billion."

11
Advertising the Global Image

Corporate advertising, which is designed to establish and enhance—even to change—the corporate image, is an especially effective tool in markets outside the home country. As discussed in Chapter 1, consumers and corporate clients are more likely to purchase from companies they know or about which they (rightly or wrongly) have positive images.

Why advertise the company rather than the product? For most global companies, it is a way of establishing recognition in the marketplace. The London-based pollster Market & Opinion Research International (MORI) has shown that, in general, the better a company is known, the more highly it is regarded. "There are exceptions to this rule, of course," notes Robert Worcester, president of MORI. "In the United Kingdom, for example, most nationalized industries and most car companies are prominent but relatively poorly regarded. In Germany, we find that the car industry is well regarded, while the oil industry is much more critically viewed. In general, though, as a company becomes more familiar, it will tend to be better regarded."

More companies appear to be recognizing this fact since corporate advertising (focusing on the company image rather than on specific products) is on the increase. According to the *Public Relations Journal,* corporate advertising is up 11.5 percent, to nearly $1.4 billion—outpacing overall advertising expenditures for 1989. Among the top 10 corporate spenders that year were Sears, Ford Motor, Chrysler, Campeau, IBM, General Electric, and General Motors.

"We believe that the ultimate function of corporate communications is to convince the audience that a company's management knows what it is doing and where it is going—that management has a vision. Product advertising alone won't do that," explains James Foster, president and CEO of Brouillard Communications, a division of J. Walter Thompson Co. "On the contrary, in the era of rampant takeovers, management must be on the alert for any situation in which the company's various parts may be judged to be worth more than the whole."

Guidelines for Successful Advertising

According to Brouillard Communications, there are a few points worth keeping in mind for producing a good corporate advertising program:

1. *Look ahead.* Ads that merely boast about a company's financial record can be boring. While there is nothing wrong with presenting a company's record, it should almost never be the main point. Instead, focus on where the company is headed.

2. *Try to epitomize the company in a single powerful thought.* An advertising campaign that cuts through the clutter and gets results will discuss its business philosophy, what its strengths are, and where it hopes to go. Providing a relatively simple conceptual picture of the company is the goal.

3. *Don't make a mountain out of a molehill.* Some corporate advertising focuses on products or projects that have reader appeal but that represent a tiny percentage of the company's net income. This may be legitimate when it is clearly done to indicate a possibility. It is dead wrong when done with an implication that the "one percenter" will have a significant impact on near-term earnings. All that will accomplish is to alienate the audience it is supposed to impress.

4. *Remember that the message sent is not necessarily the message received.* It is vital to plan an ad campaign and get the strategy right. But don't make the mistake of believing that good advertising is as simple as summarizing the strategy and calling it an ad. The message sent is not necessarily the message received. Successful advertising involves the art of translating the strategy into a stimulus that will get the desired response. There is no substitute for the knowledge and talent it takes to do this.

5. *Speak with a single voice.* In taking a multimedia approach, don't scatter your shot. Make sure that the various media you use are all delivering the same basic message. Remember the need for a simple, conceptual picture of your company (see item 2 above). The most difficult form of unity is probably tone of voice. This refers not to what you say, but to how

you say it. For example, should your communications be spirited and openly optimistic, or sober and conservative? The answer depends in part on management style. Your written and visual communications should create the same feeling that management creates in face-to-face meetings. This kind of consistency builds confidence.

The following case studies illustrate why the decision is made to undertake an advertising campaign spotlighting the company. ABB (Asea Brown Boveri) is intent on establishing itself as the boundaryless corporation; Toyota, Honda, and Fujitsu want to appear less threatening in the sometimes hostile U.S. market.

Case Example

ABB: Introducing the New Kid on the Block

The main purpose of this company's communications efforts has been to let the world know what ABB is and what it can do globally. The cornerstone of the communications program has been a multimillion-dollar corporate advertising campaign. While layout and copy may vary slightly from country to country, "the basic message is that we are a global company, but that we act local," says ABB's Senior Vice President of Corporate Information Heinz Haussmann. "At most airports you will see posters like that. The present advertising underlines the fact that we are not just an electrical-engineering company, but that a big part of our business is in environmental technology." (For a sample of such an advertisement, see Figure 11-1.)

Getting the Message Across.   Recent data reveal that the target audience is apparently getting the message. Comments Haussmann: "You have to take into account, of course, our special situation. ABB is only three years old. In the first one or two years, the only thing we had to do was to create awareness of who we were and what we were doing. The research data that just came in suggest that we very much have obtained our objective. There are good indications that our key audiences, such as utilities and governments, understand who we are, what we are doing, and where we are doing it. Of course, it's not the same in every country, but generally I think we are quite satisfied that we are on the right track."

The company also keeps an eye on its global image when dealing with the media. "We are trying to come away from the label the press is always giving us as a Swedish–Swiss company, which is not true. For instance, we have our big international press conferences in many capitals of the world, not just in Zurich. We do press seminars in many different places internationally and carefully select key executives from

**The art
of being local
worldwide.**

We'd like to   wish our customers, business partners, and the
communities we serve a happy and prosperous New Year.
          Our business—and yours—is the clean, economical
generation of electrical power, getting it to where
people need it, and its efficient use in industry, transportation,
environmental control, and other key sectors.
          We look forward to sharing the challenges and opportunities
of 1991, and continuing a tradition of partnership and friendly
service that began over 100 years ago.
          We are at home wherever you, our partners, need us—in
over 140 countries. That's the art of being local worldwide.

Figure 11-1

around the world for interviews in the media so that we get an international coverage," explains Haussmann.

He adds that the corporate advertising will continue even after ABB is no longer seen as the new kid on the block. "You have to keep the attention, awareness, and understanding alive. If you don't advertise and everybody else does, you lose the kind of awareness and understanding that we have now."

Case Example

Toyota: Humanizing the Corporate Image

All too often, the image a large global corporation projects is that of an uncaring, faceless organization concerned only with its profit line. The problem is even more pervasive, however, for Japanese corporations. Even though they are usually viewed by Americans as manufacturers of some of the highest-quality goods, Japanese firms are often stereotyped as cold, mechanized, unfeeling entities. The challenge for them is to put the people side of the business into the picture. To this end, Toyota has developed its first corporate advertising campaign in an attempt to humanize the company.

Toyota's current campaign in the print media focuses on the positive role of the company in the various communities in which it operates. The ads for the most part concentrate on the successes of various charitable activities Toyota supports, but one ad addresses the benefit a town is receiving from Toyota's tax revenues. Although the company denies that the campaign was developed in direct response to anti-Japanese sentiment, the overall message—that Toyota is a local player that contributes to the social and economic well-being of America—certainly addresses many of the complaints of U.S. Japan-bashers.

Research on public perceptions of the Japanese automaker helped guide Toyota to the conclusion that a corporate ad campaign was needed. "The research showed that we were very strong in product-related traits," explains Tim Andree, manager of Toyota's Public Relations Group. "We've almost cornered the market on quality, reliability, and dependability. However, we felt there's this whole other side that we think is necessary to explain."

Getting Personal.   Andree describes the strategy behind the advertising: "People knew our product, but they knew it at a time when it could largely be considered something that was imported and brought in from the outside. Well, that situation is slowly and gradually, but substantially, changing. Toyota is a product that's being made here by Americans, and our American operations are growing. In order to explain that, I think it might be natural that a company would use corporate advertising.

"I believe people now realize we make cars in America," he says, "but still they don't really know Toyota beyond the product. This [advertising] effort is telling stories that we hope will help people know us a little bit better and understand us a little better as people."

The accounts given in the ads portray Toyota as a group of caring individuals who do more than just make quality automobiles. "The stories are very appealing," says Andree. "They benefit the organizations we support and also open the door a little, give a little glimmer of light about what kind of people work at Toyota here in America, and what kind of corporate philosophies run the company. They show that beyond the product, beyond the good cars that everyone knows really well, there are a lot of human faces." (For a sample of the Toyota ad campaign, see Figures 11-2 and 11-3.)

The strategy has certain drawbacks, however. "What Toyota is doing is more aggressive than what most other international firms do in tying their corporate citizenship to their advertising," says Alan Parter, president of Parter International, a communications consulting firm that specializes in international companies doing business in the United States.

"Clearly, there are benefits in that they are drawing attention to their good works," he observes. "But there's also a danger. Japanese philanthropy is viewed with much greater skepticism and it's often thought of as more self-serving than the philanthropy U.S. companies do, whether that's fair or not. So Toyota has to be *extremely* careful that its advertising doesn't appear self-serving."

Doing Business in the United States.   "In general," says Parter, "the Japanese feel less comfortable than Americans do with patting themselves on the back and promoting their good works. I think there's a cultural inclination there to let good deeds speak for themselves. So this [ad campaign] is unusual for a Japanese company, unless it's because Toyota sees itself as an American company now and therefore is telling the public what's going on."

Andree confirms this, stressing that the campaign was not necessarily designed as a reply to Japan-bashing. "While we're a company that is Japanese rooted, [the campaign] is not in response to anything. This is really just a natural outgrowth of our American operations. American companies do corporate advertising also, and they do it because they have substantial operations here. Toyota has substantial operations here, and therefore we're communicating to the community.

"We're just telling people what we do besides build good cars," he continues. "Our presence in America has grown substantially in the past 10 years. We're designing cars; we're doing a great deal of the R&D for our products here. We're also manufacturing a substantial number of cars here. Therefore, we're employing more people and moving into a lot of communities. And when you move into communities, you have an obligation and a responsibility not only to contribute to the community by employing people and being a good business, but you have a responsibility to explain yourself, explain what you're like, and explain the kinds of things you believe in."

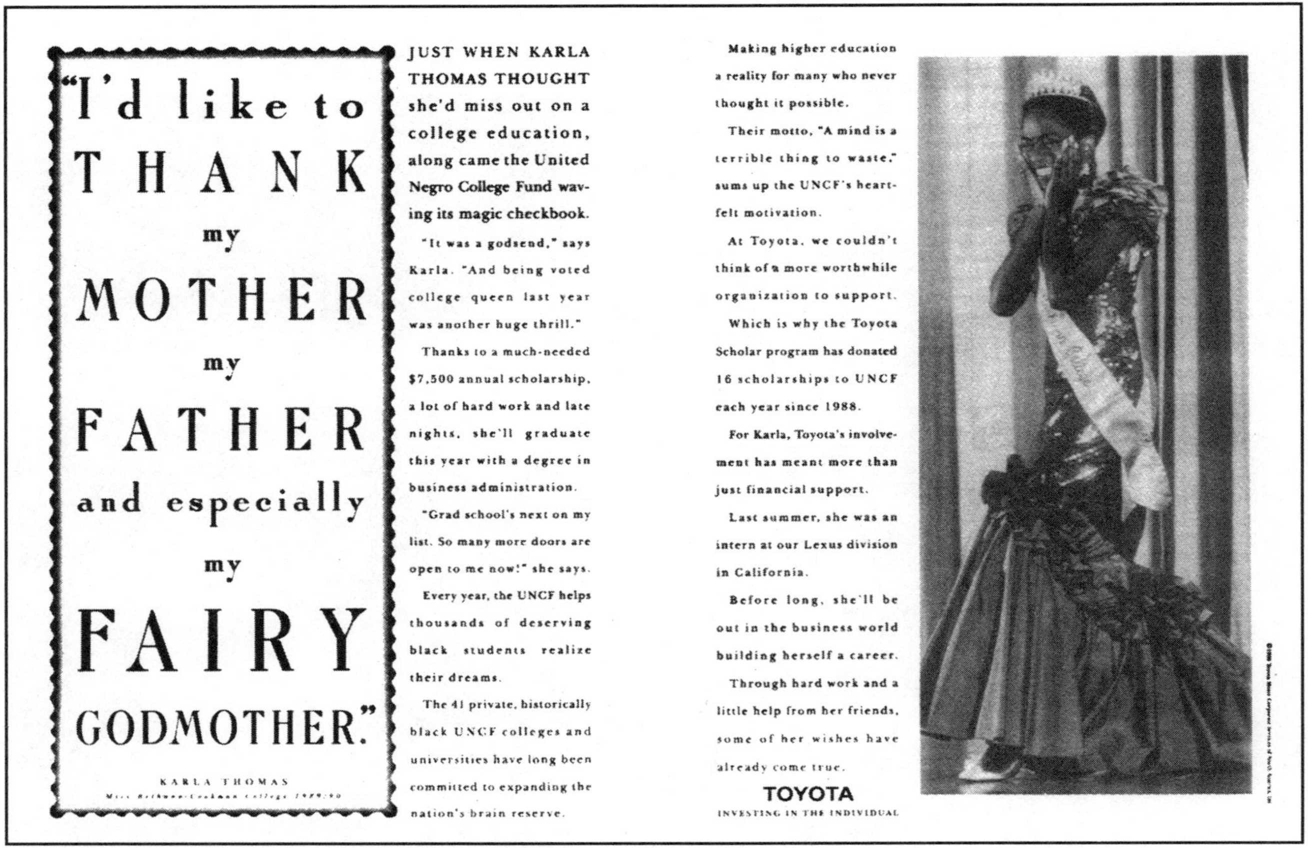
"I'd like to THANK my MOTHER my FATHER and especially my FAIRY GODMOTHER."
KARLA THOMAS
JUST WHEN KARLA THOMAS THOUGHT she'd miss out on a college education, along came the United Negro College Fund waving its magic checkbook.
"It was a godsend," says Karla. "And being voted college queen last year was another huge thrill."
Thanks to a much-needed $7,500 annual scholarship, a lot of hard work and late nights, she'll graduate this year with a degree in business administration.
"Grad school's next on my list. So many more doors are open to me now!" she says.
Every year, the UNCF helps thousands of deserving black students realize their dreams.
The 41 private, historically black UNCF colleges and universities have long been committed to expanding the nation's brain reserve.
Making higher education a reality for many who never thought it possible.
Their motto, "A mind is a terrible thing to waste," sums up the UNCF's heartfelt motivation.
At Toyota, we couldn't think of a more worthwhile organization to support.
Which is why the Toyota Scholar program has donated 16 scholarships to UNCF each year since 1988.
For Karla, Toyota's involvement has meant more than just financial support.
Last summer, she was an intern at our Lexus division in California.
Before long, she'll be out in the business world building herself a career.
Through hard work and a little help from her friends, some of her wishes have already come true.
TOYOTA
INVESTING IN THE INDIVIDUAL

Figure 11-2

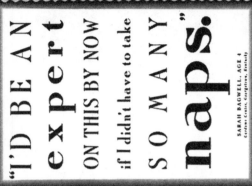
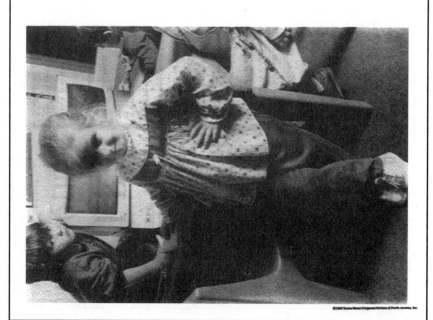
Figure 11-3

He continues: "I think what the ads do is show that we share values with a lot of the organizations we support. We want to put those organizations in the limelight, and hopefully that will lead other people to support them also."

The campaign, which began in May 1990, has no scheduled ending date. "This isn't something where we're just trying to push a few buttons and then stop," says Andree. "This is a communications effort. We have things to tell and we will continue to use this medium to do it." That same attitude pervades the whole communications approach: "There are several activities that we're involved in but there isn't really any grand scheme. This is really what we are. We're just trying to be as credible and sincere as possible and show what we are. And when we have the opportunity to do that we'll make use of the appropriate medium at the time."

Toyota's corporate-image efforts, however, address the specific situation in the United States and are not appropriate for other Toyota markets not as developed as the United States. For instance, the company's first wholly owned manufacturing facility in the United Kingdom is only now going up. "To some degree," says Andree, "I can see that they're behind the extent of the operations in the United States. We started our operations in the United States in 1957; we've been here a long time. To start a corporate ad campaign in 1990 after being here 33 years or so is something that came out of our long experience here and the growth of our operations. I think it's going to take a while to start something like that in the United Kingdom or in Europe."

Case Example

Honda: Overcoming the "Outsiders" Stigma

The biggest image problem for the average Japanese company trying to do business in the United States results from its being Japanese. As anti-Japanese sentiment increases in the media, in the political arena, and on street corners, many Japanese corporations are grappling with the question of how to make Americans more comfortable with their presence and how to overcome the stigma of being "outsiders." In few industries is this issue more sensitive than in the auto industry.

As American as Apple Pie. Honda has responded by attempting to make the United States public more aware of its American manufacturing operations. American Honda Motor Co. has been producing motorcycles in the United States since 1979 and automobiles since 1982; it currently employs more than 40,000 U.S. workers. What's more, the Accord coupe, one of America's top-selling cars, is made only in the United States, and thousands of them are exported to Japan every year.

"We don't try to overemphasize 'Made in the USA,' " says Bob Butorac, American Honda's assistant manager of corporate public relations. "But certainly we try to let the public know that Honda has made substantial investments in the United States and that we do have a long-term commitment toward doing business in this country. We try to stress not only sales, but the fact that we manufacture in the United States; the fact that we're not just assembling cars here, but that we're building cars almost from the ground up."

Print Advertising. At the center of this effort is a corporate print advertising campaign (part of which can be seen in Figure 11-4). "Basically, it's designed to give a little bit better picture to a lot of people as to Honda's commitment and involvement within the U.S. economy," says Eric Conn, senior manager of auto advertising for American Honda. "In this ad we talk about cars designed and built in America being exported to other countries—a discussion on the balance of trade."

The campaign strategy aims at three target audiences: "acceptors," "convertibles," and "influentials." Acceptors are people who have already bought Japanese products. In their case, the ads simply serve to reinforce their purchase decisions and remind them that they did contribute to the U.S. economy. The second group, convertibles, are people who are "sort of on the fence," explains Conn. "They don't refuse to buy Japanese products—they're aware of them, they know the qualities—but there's still a little red, white, and blue tug at their heart. Hopefully with these people you can show them that this is a return of investment into the United States. A Honda is not an off-shore product in the traditional sense. We want them to climb off the fence and come join us." The last group, influentials, consists of business and government leaders, educators, and some enthusiasts. "These people have a major influence over others' decisions—they're often looked to for advice. So obviously we'd want to remind them that we're part of the economy and get them on our side a little bit."

"It's a smart idea," says communications consultant Alan Parter. "Japanese companies have suffered a lot of negative press and bad feelings in this country, and one of the major complaints is that they export more than they import. This advertising relates specifically to those business concerns and answers those criticisms."

The campaign began only in December 1990, but Honda's response to anti-Japanese sentiments has been in the works for some time. The idea has been on the back burner while the company reorganized and centralized its U.S. management. "It's sort of an internal structure thing," says Conn. "We've been aware for quite a while that we needed a campaign like this, but it just took us a while to really get ourselves centralized and get a cohesive agreement on a sense of direction. We have all these different elements within our company, all the different divisions. We finally really got ourselves organized internally. Now there is one central management group, Honda North America, to which all the different groups report."

What's right with this picture?

You won't see very many Accord Coupes that look like this one. There is no question about that. Unless, of course, you happen to work at Honda's factory located in Marysville, Ohio. Or live in Japan.

Carefully built and assembled at one of the automotive industry's most advanced manufacturing facilities, the Accord Coupe is made only in America. But that's not the only place it's sold.

Thousands of new Accord Coupes are exported to Japan each and every year. Where they are prized for their engineering, craftsmanship and value. Just as they are here.

But the other reason the Japanese are fond of this car is because it comes with right-hand drive. Which is fitting since they drive on the opposite side of the road in Japan.

Mind you, producing both right-hand and left-hand drive cars from the same assembly line takes a lot of extra effort. The fact that Honda is the only U.S. carmaker to do so speaks for itself.

It's this kind of innovation and true commitment to people's needs which makes Honda, well, Honda.

Because even though we sell more Accord Coupes in America, it's just as important to satisfy our customers in other parts of the world.

After all, when you look at the big picture, that's what it's all about.

HONDA

Figure 11-4

Media Communications.   Honda's press relations department has been emphasizing the contribution of its U.S. operations for several years. "We had a press event when we first started exporting cars to Japan in 1988 that was very well attended and received a lot of coverage," says Butorac. "And that was really the first time we talked in a big way about Honda exporting cars from the United States to other nations."

The Accord station wagon was introduced in December 1990 in Marysville, Ohio, for two reasons. As Butorac explains: "Number one, that's the only place in the world where that car is being built. Number two, we wanted to bring home the development side of the story of that car because the engineering and the design—even the making of the dyes to stamp out the parts—all that was done here in the United States by Honda."

The introduction was essentially a two-day press conference that featured not only the new car, but also the American Honda Motor Co. manufacturing and the Honda R&D capabilities that were established in Ohio. Notes Butorac: "The chief designers from our California studio also talked about the styling and what they've accomplished and how their operation has developed over the years. They then used the wagon as an illustration of that. So in addition to a regular product story or a regular business story, we try to make that type of information available."

Will It Work?   While it's probably too early to say definitively how well the communications plan is paying off, Honda says the preliminary results are promising. "I think awareness has improved, especially among opinion leaders, that Honda has made such a large commitment to the U.S. market and has made so many contributions to this country, economically and technologically," says Butorac. "I believe I can safely say that the research indicated that among opinion leaders there definitely had been a growing awareness."

Although Honda has a slight advantage over many other Japanese firms because it has had a U.S. presence a little longer, it knows there are still limits to how far it can Americanize itself in the minds of U.S. consumers. "Honda's been around since the '60s," says Conn, "so we're a *little* different. We are a little better known—some of our attributes as to product quality, reliability, dependability, are helping *separate* us from the crowd. But nonetheless, we're still obviously perceived as a Japanese company. As long as it says 'Honda' on the door it'll always be a Japanese company. We're kidding ourselves if we try to go too far. We're doing a tremendous amount of things in America, making a tremendous contribution and investing a lot of money, but that will never take away the origin of the company."

Case Example

Fujitsu: Adjusting an Image to a Wider Market

Since its founding 56 years ago, Fujitsu Ltd. has grown from being a small Japanese manufacturer of telephone-switching systems to a

$16 billion global technology corporation with operations in 25 countries around the world. As it has grown, Fujitsu has tried to center its image around the fact that it is a global player. The sign-off on all of its corporate advertising touts Fujitsu as "the *global* computer and communications company." However, as Fujitsu's technology begins to reach new markets, the company has started reexamining its image and looking at ways to make it more relevant to its expanding consumer base.

The Global Campaign. Fujitsu's corporate ad campaign, running since 1986, now features a series of stories about various business applications for which Fujitsu products have been used. Although the company's advertising efforts are somewhat decentralized, similar ads run all over the world, with the stories tailored to local markets. David Gould, vice president of corporate communication for Fujitsu America Inc., explains that the basic purpose for the campaign was to build awareness of the company name. "We are not a well-known global company," says Gould. "Most people are surprised to find out that we're the second-largest data-processing company in the world behind IBM."

The campaign was designed to "put a face on the company," according to Gould. "The slogan itself represented the company's internal desire to globalize its operation and to reflect on the fact that Fujitsu is not just a Japanese company, it's truly a global company. For the first two years, the ads featured Fujitsu employees in an effort to give people the sense that we're really Americans working for this company. We're not just eight Japanese guys using an 800 telephone number from some factory in New Jersey selling disc drives. The ads told the story about how our employees were contributing significantly to the success of the U.S. business investment. And they were able to do this knowing that there was a huge global company behind them. In Europe, similar ads are run using their own local applications." (For a sample of the ad campaign, see Figure 11-5.)

Over the past several years, Fujitsu has been gradually diversifying its business away from its tradition of original equipment manufacturing to production of more branded products. "We've changed to a company where about one-third of our U.S. revenues are now end-user products with the Fujitsu name on them," says Gould. Thus, increasing awareness of the name has become even more important. "This campaign was really designed to build, within the corporate business world, the idea that Fujitsu was a major player. It has a tremendous capability in terms of global resources in the technology area. When you do business with a Fujitsu person, you have this huge global company standing behind you that can fill all of your data-processing, computer, and communications needs. That was the basic strategy over the last five years."

The global image is important to Fujitsu because it is significant to its customers, who are often high-level managers considering purchasing huge integrated systems for their companies. "To the CEO of a large corporation, our being global is very important," says Gould, "because if he had to choose between us and another major company, and he didn't

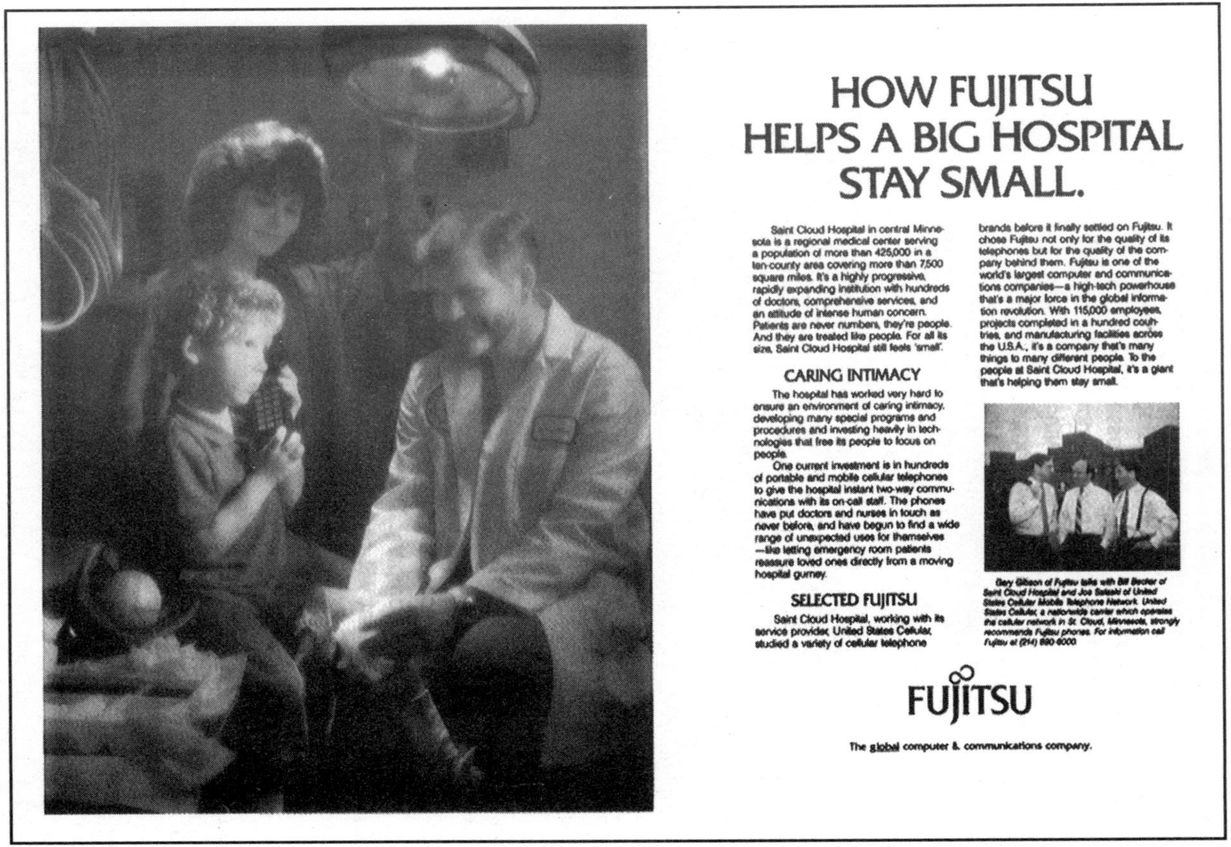
HOW FUJITSU
HELPS A BIG HOSPITAL
STAY SMALL.
Saint Cloud Hospital in central Minnesota is a regional medical center serving a population of more than 425,000 in a ten-county area covering more than 7,500 square miles. It's a highly progressive, rapidly expanding institution with hundreds of doctors, comprehensive services, and an attitude of intense human concern. Patients are never numbers, they're people. And they are treated like people. For all its size, Saint Cloud Hospital still feels 'small.'
CARING INTIMACY
The hospital has worked very hard to ensure an environment of caring intimacy, developing many special programs and procedures and investing heavily in technologies that free its people to focus on people.
One current investment is in hundreds of portable and mobile cellular telephones to give the hospital instant two-way communications with its on-call staff. The phones have put doctors and nurses in touch as never before, and have begun to find a wide range of unexpected uses for themselves —like letting emergency room patients reassure loved ones directly from a moving hospital gurney.
SELECTED FUJITSU
Saint Cloud Hospital, working with its service provider, United States Cellular, studied a variety of cellular telephone brands before it finally settled on Fujitsu. It chose Fujitsu not only for the quality of its telephones but for the quality of the company behind them. Fujitsu is one of the world's largest computer and communications companies—a high-tech powerhouse that's a major force in the global information revolution. With 115,000 employees, projects completed in a hundred countries, and manufacturing facilities across the U.S.A., it's a company that's many things to many different people. To the people at Saint Cloud Hospital, it's a giant that's helping them stay small.
FUJITSU
The global computer & communications company.

Figure 11-5

know that we were truly a global company and very big, he's not going to choose us. So there's a very important message there."

He continues: "When a top senior manager buys a system from us, whether it's an automated teller machine, a point-of-sale system, or a PBX product, those are major investments a company makes in technology—they're not just buying a box. They're adapting all of their internal MIS or telecommunication systems to our product line. Therefore, it's reassuring for a manager to know that there's a global company putting global resources into the technology; and the R&D that goes into the product is reassuring, too. I think all of those things are important. It provides elimination of risk."

Perhaps one of the best examples of Fujitsu's efforts to promote its image as a global firm is its corporate logo, which was revised in 1989. Previously, the Fujitsu name had been spelled in Roman characters for the American market and in kanji for the Japanese. Now, however, the company sports a single logo worldwide, with the name spelled in Roman characters. "That's a direct reflection of the company positioning itself as a global company," says Gould. He cautions that Fujitsu is not trying to downplay its Japanese origins, though. "You can't run away from it," he says. "Fujitsu is a Japanese name. One of the things that was considered was whether initials should be used, like FJT Corp. or something. But that wasn't done. There's a lot of equity in the fact that the company has a tremendous history. Why walk away from the name when it has worked for 50 years?"

Fujitsu's communications efforts have paid off, but there is room for improvement. "The ads test well; people recall them," says Gould. "But we still have a lot of work. I think the fact that there's a lot to do in building name awareness is not necessarily a reflection of the advertising itself, but maybe of the fact that we're not out there enough getting the message out in a competitive way with other companies of our size. Once people know us, we are in most cases able to forge very strong business relationships. Although no one is going to say, 'I learned about this company in an ad,' we hope that if people see our ads in business publications, they'll at least build up a contextual understanding of our company and its products."

Time for a Change.   As the cost of Fujitsu's technology has come down over the past year and a half, it has become accessible to a much wider market. The company must now adjust its image to address the concerns not only of top managers and operations departments but of other business consumers. These include both entrepreneurs and the purchasing departments of large corporations that draw up lists of approved products. "If a fax machine or a printer is needed," says Gould, "they call up our purchasing department and ask about the approved list. They can then specify the kind of product they want to buy. Therefore, awareness of the brand name is really important; if they've never heard of Fujitsu, they're not going to choose it."

Customers Want Reliability. For business consumers, knowledge of the brand name is important, but quality, reliability, and service are much more relevant issues than whether or not the producer is a global company. Therefore, Fujitsu is in the process of developing a new ad campaign that will give greater play to the local adaptability of its products. According to Gould: "When you get to support staff—a secretary specifying, for example, a fax machine or a printer for the office from an approved purchasing list—this person is not really concerned if it's a global company or not. They're going to buy based more on things a nonbusiness consumer would: name recognition, important product attributes, quality. I think our new advertising is going to reflect that."

Jean Boddewyn, professor of marketing and international business at Baruch College in New York City, agrees with the new tactic: "The significance of the global message depends a great deal on the product and the audience. Maybe it's important to consumers that companies such as Federal Express or DHL are global and that they deliver to many different countries. But for a product such as Campbell's soup, the average housewife buying the product doesn't really care if it's sold all around the world or not."

The new advertising will also stress Fujitsu's whole line of products. Gould explains: "People know us for a specific product line right now, for example, 'Fujitsu, the fax company.' But if you ask if they're aware of any other products we manufacture, more often than not they say 'no.' Or they might say, 'Oh, you make PBX machines' or 'You make disc drives.' But no one says, 'You make a lot of things.' And that's the message that we need to get out.

"We're finding that when we go into a company, one of our key advantages is that we sell many different products. When people come into a specific kind of product, they're also coming into a *company*, and we want them to know that that company is going to have various solutions for them. Therefore, our advertising will have to take more of a product family view. We don't want to be known just as a fax company or a PBX company. We want to be known as a company that offers a wide range of solutions. 'There's a lot more to Fujitsu than you really know' is the message."

12

Protecting the Corporate Image: The Trend in Consumer Activism

Boycotts have gained prominence—especially in the United States—as a means for consumer groups to express their opposition to certain corporate practices. They are often viewed as an effective means of getting companies' attention because they not only threaten the company's bottom line, but also its corporate image. Furthermore, a diminished image can create long-term internal problems for companies, hurting morale, and making it difficult to recruit good employees. While most people still do not take part in boycotts, those who do tend to be prime corporate marketing targets: generally well educated, affluent, and young. For this reason, companies must develop a policy to manage their response to boycotts (see following box for ways to use industry groups to deal with consumer pressures).

The Growth of Boycotts

Although governments and small companies have been drawn into the battle, global corporations face the greatest public relations challenge from boycotts. With the list of possible "crimes" growing longer every day, the bigger and more successful a company, the more likely it is to be accused of

Joint Industry Efforts Dealing with Global Critics

Consultation is replacing confrontation as the chief tactic in corporate efforts to fend off multilateral constraints on their operational autonomy. Mindful that the fractured corporate response to the infant-formula controversy helped lead to an unwelcome global marketing code (established by the UN), many companies are now participating in industrywide programs to deal with common external pressures and provide an alternative to the imposition of similar forms of regulation.

The decision to forge industry associations usually works best if the consequences of inaction are clearly understood. Companies must be able to uncover a single, mutual, overriding problem on which their future profitability depends. The issue must be too large to be managed in the conventional context of contract negotiations or through the bilateral diplomatic channels of home and host country governments. For example, an industry-sponsored program to assist 28 Latin American governments with the development of safe pesticide rules was implemented only after it became apparent that foreign-based chemical manufacturers would lose their market share in a wave of antipesticide hysteria.

The following checklist is based on examples of corporate cooperation in the pharmaceutical and agrochemical industries. It covers key points to consider in framing a plan to facilitate cooperation with others, to establish consensus, and to negotiate mutually enforceable agreements.

- *Carefully examine the challenges facing your industry.* Although participation in industry cooperative efforts has definite benefits, there are also potential risks. The companies will have to make both financial and time commitments. Furthermore, initial dialogue may result in larger concessions than originally intended, either to others in the industry or to those on the other side of the negotiating table. Also, any credible plan of action by industry will likely involve the release of considerable amounts of technological and marketing data. Some companies, for competitive reasons, may wish to provide this information on their own terms or withhold it entirely.

- *Establish clearly the limits of cooperation before framing a plan of action.* Many industry-backed efforts have foundered because of misunderstandings as to whether activities will be voluntary or binding. If the industry's objective is goodwill and a simple communication of perspectives, this should be made clear to the relevant spokesperson for the other side.

In deciding the limits of their commitment, companies should be aware that one of the key virtues of the voluntary approach is its feasibility. It works best when both sides are polarized. On the other hand, binding negotiations may be necessary to constituencies. Choosing between the two formats is useful in defining what the business community intends to accomplish and how much it is willing to sacrifice to gain it.

- *Avoid hidden traps in setting an agenda.*   One common mistake is to embark on a program of "fact finding" and use the results to establish priorities. The "found" facts may actually exacerbate conflicts and lead to unproductive hardening of perspectives.

  Developing an informal agreement on the dimensions of the problem should always come first, followed by research, exchange of opinions on various solutions, and, last, formulation of the consensus position itself.

- *Limit participation—from both sides—to decision makers.*   High-level executives are usually more skilled in the art of the possible and can easily commit their companies to a proposed course of action. An effort must be made at the outset to attract officials who can speak with authority and approve an initiative without extensive delay. The size of the negotiation group should be kept to a minimum.

- *Ensure that discussions are private.*   Use of a public forum has proved disastrous. It encourages self-indulgent grandstanding and contributes to rigidity in the presentation of ideas.

some form of corporate "irresponsibility." The longer-range intent of many boycott organizers is to have a negative economic impact on the company involved. But the immediate goal is usually to generate negative publicity and to raise the level of public awareness of an issue.

A poll conducted last summer by Peter D. Hart Associates for Americans for Constitutional Freedom reveals that even in the United States, only a small portion of the public has been involved in boycotts, but a clear majority believe in their right to participate. Environmental issues were identified by the poll as the most common reason for support of a company boycott. Another popular area for boycotts, both in the United States and in Europe, is animal rights. At present, there are anywhere from 200 to 300 boycotts sponsored or actively supported by more than 70 consumer, environmental, and political groups.

Consumer activists now have a publication that lists boycott activities. This Seattle-based report, *National Boycott News* (NBN), is also useful for corporations wishing to stay on top of the boycott movement. According to NBN editor Todd Putnam, the publication focuses on reporting and detailed analyses of boycott activity (the most recent background issue ran 194 pages). It covers not only current boycotts, but also boycott success stories, includes company replies to boycotters, and, in addition, highlights products boycott supporters *should* buy.

The Issues of Major Boycotts

In order for companies to respond to boycotts, they must stay on top of the issues that are of interest to consumers (see Chapter 8 for a discussion of issue tracking). Recently, boycott movements have been activated by a number of issues. These have included the environment, peace, labor, human rights/political rights, health care, and animal rights. While the majority of boycotts have occurred in the United States, their spread to other consumer markets is to be expected.

The following discussion covers some of the major focuses of consumer activism. Although the issues covered below are diverse, companies should note that the methods used by consumer groups to attract a broader following are fairly similar.

Environment

The environment as an issue is gaining popular support across the globe. While in the United States, environmental activism has not been as strong as in Asia and Europe, certainly as public awareness increases, boycotts are to be expected. In anticipation, companies are developing image campaigns to depict themselves as "friends of the environment" (see Chapter 7).

In Asia, the rapid pace of industrialization is fueling environmental movements. In South Korea, for example, Coca-Cola, Eastman Kodak, Kentucky Fried Chicken, Anheuser-Busch, Seagram, Nestlé, 3M, and Kiewit Continental Can face the largest consumer boycott in recent memory. They are all affiliated with the Doosan Group in South Korea, which has been accused of leaking chlorophenol into the Naktong River. Grass-roots activists have initiated a boycott against the Doosan Group's best-known consumer products—items made by local and foreign-invested joint ventures with no connection to Doosan Electro-Materials, which was held responsible for the leaks. Hardest hit by the boycott were Doosan's own products, such as OB beer (made by the Oriental Brewery) and Doosan Dairy milk.

Peace Movement

- *Infact.* Several companies have been under siege from antiwar activists. One of the best-known campaigns is Boston-based Infact's boycott of General Electric (GE). (Infact rose to prominence because of its efforts in the Nestlé infant formula boycott of 1977–84.) Infact launched a boycott of GE in June 1986 to protest that company's involvement in the U.S. defense industry. A central element of Infact's campaign is to show that GE controls U.S. defense policy by conceiving new nuclear systems, advocating military strategies and national policies that legitimize such systems, and lobbying through government and business ties to secure defense contracts.

  In its tightly constructed grass-roots approach, its ties to other corporate critic groups, and its protest tactics, Infact is a model of how a company-focused boycott organization operates. Infact claims to be having an economic impact on GE. It has applied its boycott at the institutional level to hospital purchases of GE medical equipment and to retailers' product choices. However, while Infact contends that sales have decreased in the areas of consumer products, medical equipment, and building projects, for a total of $57.4 million in lost sales for the company, GE representatives say that the overall economic impact of the boycott has been negligible.

- *Other organizations.* Other companies and products have also been targeted by the peace movement. These include (1) a boycott of products made by the Providence, Rhode Island-based manufacturer Hasbro, called by the New England War Resisters League; (2) a boycott of Morton Salt, AT&T, and the top 50 companies in the defense industry, called by Nuclear Free America (NFA); and (3) a boycott of all French-made products by a group called Worldwide Nuclear Freeze.

  Based in Baltimore, the NFA has a data-base project that lists contracts of Department of Defense contractors for nuclear weapons and nuclear weapons systems. The NFA asks its supporters not to invest in or purchase products made by the 50 largest nuclear weapons contractors. It is also the foremost advocate of nuclear-free zones. At last count, the NFA reported 168 towns and counties in the United States that have declared themselves nuclear-free zones, for a worldwide total of 4407 zones in 23 countries. The NFA is participating in Infact's GE boycott.

Health Care

- *The Nestlé boycott revisited.* The boycott of Nestlé products from 1977–84, to protest the marketing and distribution of infant formula in less-developed countries (LDCs), was one of the first highly publicized activist boycotts to single out an MNC. It also served as a precedent for similar boycotts that sprouted up in the 1980s. Although Infact ended the boycott in 1984, Action for Corporate Accountability (Action)—an off-shoot of Infact—called for a renewal of the boycott in 1988. Adding American Home Products (AHP) to the boycott, Action claims that Nestlé and AHP continue with improper marketing practices by "dumping" free infant formula in LDC hospitals.

Action says that it has received active support for the boycott in 20 countries. Through its membership in the International Baby Food Action Network (Ibfan) of the Organization of Consumer Unions (IOCU), it has regular contacts with health workers in 70 countries. Action experienced organizational difficulties last year with the loss of its director, and the boycott is being run largely by Action Associate Director Carol-Linnea Salmon.

According to the 1990 edition of Ibfan's *Breaking the Rules,* put together by Action and edited by Salmon, the Nestlé/AHP boycott has been endorsed by groups in 67 countries through the formation (at Ibfan's 1989 Manila Conference) of the International Nestlé Boycott Alliance.

■ *Antismoking maneuvers.*   Tobacco companies have been the targets of a campaign urging institutions to divest themselves of tobacco stocks. Last spring, Harvard University and the City University of New York disclosed they had sold their stock in large tobacco companies such as Philip Morris. The Tobacco Divestment Project, a newly created antismoking group based in Boston, plans to keep pressing major institutional investors, such as insurance companies and hospitals, to join the crusade.

Tobacco companies may soon be under attack from another kind of boycott. Antismoking groups, heartened by the success of the tuna boycott (see "Animal Rights," following), may soon move from encouraging stock divestment to calling for a nationwide consumer boycott of tobacco companies' food products.

Human Rights

■ *South Africa.*   Boycotts against Shell and Coca-Cola have been in effect since 1986. The two most active boycotts to target specific companies for their continued business presence in South Africa, they reached their zenith from 1986–88 and have since settled into the U.S. antiapartheid landscape.

With the change of the political scenery in South Africa since the release of Nelson Mandela in February 1990 and the start of talks between the African National Congress and the South African government, the intensity of these boycotts has lessened, although there is still pressure on companies to move out of South Africa.

The United Mine Workers of America's Boycott Shell Campaign office says that their position on South African divestment and the boycott are unchanged. However, rather than concentrating on the boycott, the anti-Shell campaign is currently placing greater attention on divestment and shareholder resolution strategies and on keeping the issue alive.

- *Operation PUSH.* Operation PUSH (People United To Serve Humanity) in the United States called for a boycott of Nike shoes in August 1990. The organization considered that Nike had made insufficient "returns to the community," based on the company's high profits from sales to minority consumers and lack of minority representation on its board or in upper management. (The lack of minority representation on the board was addressed in May 1991, with the appointment of John Thompson, the head basketball coach at Georgetown University.) Founded 20 years ago by the Reverend Jesse Jackson, Operation PUSH is a civil rights organization that seeks to advance economic development in black/minority communities, promote international peace, and improve voter registration among minorities.

Animal Rights

Boycott activity has mushroomed in recent years as a standard tactic for animal-rights groups. In the United States, the most visible animal-rights organizations are People for the Ethical Treatment of Animals, Coalition To End Animal Suffering and Exploitation, and the New England Anti-Vivisection Society. To date, the issues that have attracted most attention and received most public sympathy are the use of animal testing and treatment of laboratory animals, the fur industry, and the protection of dolphins and whales. Over the past few years, there has also been a growing tendency for animal-rights and environmental groups to endorse each other's boycotts, as was done in the boycotts of Gillette, the tuna companies, and table grapes.

Europe seems far more sophisticated in regulating animal-rights (e.g., 10 European states have signed the 1985 Convention on Animal Experimentation). Clearly, companies watching this issue closely should look to what the Europeans are doing. In many respects, the North American and Australian movements continue to follow boycott paths blazed by European groups.

- *Dolphin safety.* Last year's major newsbreaker was the decision in April by H.J. Heinz (Star-Kist), Van Kamp (Chicken of the Sea), and Bumble Bee to buy only "dolphin-safe" tuna (i.e., tuna that has been caught using techniques that do not kill dolphins). The decision was the result of a two-year boycott against tuna companies initiated by the San Francisco-based Earth Island Institute (EII), with subsequent support from an array of environmental and animal protection groups. The boycott gained strength from international networking: The EII coalesced with its Asian, European, and Latin American counterparts for strength in numbers.

The boycott is not over yet. On December 6, 1990, the EII issued a "consumer advisory" in the form of a full-page ad in three major newspapers warning that Bumble Bee was falsely claiming that its products were dolphin safe.

Bumble Bee responded to the EII's consumer advisory with its own full-page ad in *The New York Times* counterattacking the EII for misleading statements. Bumble Bee has since met with the EII and the two have agreed to work more closely on the company's dolphin-safety policy.

- *Cosmetic companies.* People for the Ethical Treatment of Animals (PETA) is the largest and most well-known animal-rights group that pressures companies to stop animal testing. As the result of the organization's efforts, Avon and Revlon announced they would stop animal testing for their cosmetic products. In 1990, PETA officially announced a joint campaign against Gillette with the New England Anti-Vivisection Society (Neavs) and the Coalition To End Animal Suffering and Exploitation. The boycott of Gillette took an interesting turn last year when several other activist groups joined the boycott and added two new issues of their own: excessive industrial waste and divestment from South Africa.

On December 17, 1990, an agreement between Gillette, PETA, and Neavs was announced, ending the four-year boycott of one of Gillette's subsidiaries, Jafra Inc. Following PETA's submission of a shareholder resolution for 1991, Gillette officials invited PETA representatives to meet with them on December 5 to discuss possible negotiations. At that meeting, Gillette agreed to a permanent ban on animal tests for Jafra cosmetics and said it would issue annual disclosures of animal test data of numbers and species used. PETA agreed to withdraw its resolution and send a representative to Gillette's April 1991 shareholder meeting to praise the company's decision and to "press for an overall corporate ban on animal tests." At the meeting, Gillette did not agree to ban testing on animals.

Religious Ideology

In the United States, two issues have prevailed over the past few years in the area of religious activism: "decency" in media advertising and television shows, and abortion rights.

- *Decency in media.* Decency in the media is generally associated with Reverend Donald Wildmon. Wildmon emerged in the late 1970s and established the National Federation for Decency (NFD). In 1987, he started a new group, Christian Leaders for Responsible Television (CleaR-TV). In 1988, he began the American Family Association (AFA) as an extension of CleaR-TV. The AFA sends a monthly newsletter to approximately 420,000 individuals and 178,000 church organizations.

  CLeaR-TV conducts prime-time viewing sweeps twice a year when it monitors new TV shows and advertisements for sex, violence, and profanity. Its boycott threats have caused advertisers to withdraw from a number of shows. Nevertheless, according to a 1989 Roper Organization study, the impact of Wildmon's activities on consumers is fairly negligible since most people are not even aware of his group. Even among those who have heard of the AFA, only a fraction can name the companies targeted by it. More important, support for this type of boycott is weak among the general public. While 20 percent of those questioned in a poll by the Americans for Constitutional Freedom had heard of the AFA, only 2 percent said they actively supported its goals (compared with 12 percent who felt "positive" about the AFA and 29 percent who strongly disagreed with it).

- *Abortion.* In the United States, abortion is an issue that hits strong nerves on both sides of the battlefield. In 1990, when AT&T decided to discontinue its $50,000 contribution to Planned Parenthood (PP), it claimed its move was based on the feeling that Planned Parenthood's "political advocacy" of the right to choose had "tainted and tarnished" AT&T's funding. AT&T's move inspired a counterattack by PP's president, Faye Wattleton, who called on PP supporters with AT&T stock to contribute it to PP for use at shareholder meetings. Prochoice activists in Minnesota also started a boycott of the retailer Dayton Hudson for its decision to withdraw an $18,000 donation to PP. Dayton Hudson eventually contributed the money to PP but it is now being boycotted by anti-abortion activists. Fear of boycotts and counterboycotts runs so strong among business that prospects in the United States for development and use of RU486—an abortion-inducing drug that also may have curative properties for some diseases—are considered dismal.

  The Christian Action Council (CAC) is one of the prolife activist groups leading the boycott of corporate sponsors of PP. The CAC prolife activities include monitoring prochoice organizations, lobbying for prolife legislation, and providing counseling services at pregnancy centers. There are now 45 companies on the CAC list, the majority of them global leaders.

Labor

Once the prime movers and innovators of boycott activity, labor no longer dominates as it did in the 1960s, 1970s, and early 1980s. With union membership dwindling in all industries, boycotts called by labor leaders are primarily those that piggyback on general issues such as health, environment, and human rights. The United Farm Workers' (UFW) boycott of grapes and lettuce is probably among the most famous of these labor campaigns.

■ *United Farm Workers.* Launched in July 1984, the United Farm Workers' (UFW) boycott of California table grapes has widened its support by refocusing the debate from workers' rights to the rational use of pesticides. Although the right to stronger unions and a more equitable collective bargaining system remain important parts of the UFW's agenda, the main thrust of the boycott emphasizes health and environmental issues. The boycott demonstrates how an old, unexploited labor issue—the occupational hazards of pesticides—can be popularized as an environmental and consumer issue.

The boycott claims to have had an economic impact on farmers. The UFW points to a USDA survey that shows sales of table grapes decreasing by 10,000 tons last year in 15 of the top markets in the United States and Canada.

Index

About the Author

THE ECONOMIST INTELLIGENCE UNIT, a wholly owned subsidiary of The Economist Group, is a publishing and research firm established to help companies initiate and maintain operations across national borders. For 45 years, it has been a source of information and know-how on worldwide business and financial developments, economic and political trends, government regulations, and corporate practice. In 1986, The Economist Intelligence Unit merged with Business International, a well-established publisher and adviser with a strong connection to multinational companies. In 1992, the EIU and BI began to publish under a single brand name: The Economist Intelligence Unit. The company maintains a global network of over 300 analysts, researchers, and editors in 95 countires. Through close working relationships with top corporate and government officials, the company analyses events and forecasts changes in the international business environment with speed and accuracy and helps companies take advantage of emerging opportunities in markets around the world.

ANDREA MACKIEWICZ is The Economist Intelligence Unit's senior editor, management practices, for the Global Management Publications Group, and an editor of the weekly report *Business International.*